Curious and Unusual Occupations

First Published in Great Britain 2021 by Mirador Publishing

First edition: 2021

A copy of this work is available through the British Library.

ISBN: 978-1-913833-82-4

Mirador Publishing
10 Greenbrook Terrace
Taunton
Somerset
TA1 1UT

Curious and Unusual Occupations An A-Z

John McKie

Contents

Alchemy

ALCHEMY IS AN ANCIENT TRADITION that was carried out in secrecy and obscurity. Its practitioners would attempt to turn lead into gold. The origin of the word "alchemy" is not clear, but it is thought to derive from the Greek word "chemis" which also occurs in the words: "chemistry" and "chemical". The practice of alchemy dates back thousands of years and the reasons for it were much more than an attempt to make easy money.

To some alchemists, gold symbolised the highest development in nature and was regarded as personifying human renewal and regeneration. The basest metal, lead, was seen as a representation of sinfulness and susceptibility to the forces of darkness. The study of alchemy is generally split into a study of its spiritual aspects, and its practical applications.

It was based in a spiritual world view in which everything that exists contains a universal spirit, meaning that metals were not only considered to be alive but to grow inside the earth. As *Lifescience.com* describes it: "To the alchemists, metals were not the unique substances that populate the Periodic Table, but instead the same thing in different stages of development or refinement."

The practice of alchemy reached its heyday in the medieval period. It was a combination of experimentation and magic. Early investigators of natural processes were centred around the search for what was known as the philosopher's stone, which they believed had supernatural properties which meant that it could heal, prolong life and change base metals into precious metals such as gold. This was a wax, liquid or powder, which had magical powers, rather than an actual stone. As *religionfacts.com* describes it: "Attempts to create the philosophers' stone were called the 'Magnum Opus', meaning 'Great Work'."

With the development of modern science, separate from religion and spirituality, belief in the transformational possibilities of alchemy went into decline, although it continued to be practised by some for centuries to come.

Alchemists believed that all elements contained the properties of fire, air, water and earth. By adjusting the proportions of these, they believed, they could make one metal into another. Gold was superior because it was thought to contain the perfect balance of all four elements.

Surprisingly, Sir Isaac Newton was a keen proponent of alchemy and wrote extensive alchemical notes throughout his lifetime. In one of these manuscripts he described how to make "philosophic mercury", a magical substance that was supposed to have the power to turn any metal into gold and even had the properties to allow one to live for ever. This is based on the fact that the process had both spiritual and practical occupations.

The practice of alchemy arose over three continents, including ancient China, India, the Greco-Roman world and the Islamic world. Western alchemy became established in Europe in the middle ages. It is thought to have derived from ancient Arabic texts and the work of Aristotle. It developed its own philosophical system and influenced many western religions. It is still unclear how much these different strands of alchemy arose independently and how much they influenced each other.

Many historians focus on European alchemy. This was based on laboratory techniques, theory, terminology and experimental method. However, it still pursued the idea of the four elements derived in antiquity. The practice was carried out in secrecy, including the use of cyphers and cryptic symbolism. Alchemists did not want their secretive practices made public, fearing that everyone would be able to carry out their work, which at least in financial terms, would render it pointless.

During the twelfth century, Robert of Chester translated an Arabic text, *The Composition of Alchemy*. Before this was done alchemy was only practised by a few people in Europe, but the translation opened the text to a much wider audience.

According to *religionfacts.com,* in the thirteenth century, Roger Bacon, an influential theologian and member of the Franciscan order, "attempted to establish a philosophical connection between alchemy and the study of Christian salvation, based on the notion of the natural turning into the supernatural". Bacon even urged Pope Clement IV to embrace the practice. "While some individual Christians did, the Church did not", *religionfacts.com* reports. As alchemy became more prevalent in Europe, many Christians voiced their opposition to it. These included Dante and Geoffrey Chaucer in the fourteenth century. In 1317, Pope John XXII issued a decree outlawing alchemy. Despite this, some Christians continued to believe in alchemy's ability to transform the natural into the supernatural and to represent the resurrection of believers.

Several women feature in the early history of alchemy. The most prominent among these is "Mary the Jewess" (c. 200 AD). She is known for her improvements to alchemy equipment and her novel methodology. Her most important discovery was the identification of hydrochloric acid, a chemical still used today. Due to the fact that many alchemists' records were anonymous, it is not possible to know how many alchemists were women. Women are absent from the historical records of alchemy in the medieval and renaissance eras, but they return in the nineteenth century as part of an occult revival of the practice.

Alchemy was doomed to fail, since it was a misunderstanding of basic rules of chemistry and physics. It was based on the theory generally accepted in the middle ages that everything in the world was based on four elements. However, it also incorporated three other substances, namely salt, mercury and sulphur. Today we know that everything is made up of atoms rather than the four elements, so attempting to adjust the proportions of these elements in a given substance is a fruitless task. However, the production process of nuclear power requires transforming one metal (uranium) into another (plutonium), so in a sense, alchemy does exist today. Additionally, with the use of particle accelerators it has proved possible to create gold out of base metals, but only in such minute quantities that the production process is not cost-efficient.

Although alchemy as it is generally known was always unsuccessful, this did not stop some of its practitioners claiming to have achieved their goal. Over the centuries, rumours abounded that the "philosopher's stone" had been created so that the transformational properties of alchemy had been achieved and that the secret of eternal life had been discovered. Since those who proclaimed this are all dead, their claims were evidently untrue. Some rich people seeking eternal life and greater riches hired alchemists to work on their behalf, but none of them were successful. Bogus alchemists who were not seriously trying to be successful in their endeavours are mentioned in Chaucer's *Canterbury Tales* and by the writer Ben Jonson.

Even though the practice of alchemy was always going to fail, the scientific community remind us that the work of alchemists in their laboratories paved the way for modern chemistry. However, it is regarded by some as an occult practice, which was revived as such during the nineteenth century.

As *lifescience.com* puts it, despite alchemy having passed into history, "the contrast between gold and lead remains. Lead is a common, poisonous metal. . . while gold is highly valued, treasured and often worn as jewellery."

Ale-Conners

AN ALE-CONNER WAS APPOINTED ANNUALLY by the manorial courts known as the Court Leets and later by local corporations, to ensure the quality and correct pricing of bread, ale and beer. The office dates back to the 1300s. There were various other terms used to describe it, for example "ale-tasters", "ale-founders" or more grandly the "Gustator Cervisiae".

The ale-conner was tasked with ensuring that the relevant foods and drinks were of good quality and sold at the statutory price. He would go from one ale house to the next, checking the quality of the beer. If the ale was found wanting, the ale-conner could take the innkeeper to the manor court to make restitution. Depending on the rules of a particular manor the ale-conner could set the price of a batch of ale or impose a fixed price for ales under the manor's jurisdiction.

With ale being such a popular tipple amongst the English, the job of the medieval ale-conner was an important one. However, it was not a sought after one. Hops were introduced to the recipe at the end of the fourteenth century by Flemish immigrants. Before the hopping process was introduced ale often went off quickly which would make the tasting unpleasant or even cause food poisoning. As a public servant and issuer of fines, the ale-conner was not always a popular member of the community. Sometimes the authorities pressed people into service for this job.

The ale-conner acted as a taxman whose job it was to ensure the beer was properly priced based on its strength and quality. It is suggested by some people that he did this, not by actually tasting the beer, but instead by sitting in a puddle of it in his regulation sturdy leather breeches. It is said that beer was poured on to a bench on which the ale-conner sat, and its strength was assessed by how sticky it seemed to be when he stood up. He would sit on the bench for half an hour and when he rose, if the beer was sticky, this was a sign it was improperly brewed. He would then impose the appropriate duty.

The ale-conner's beer quality test was designed to decide how much sugar there was in the beer. Excessive amounts of sugar were used by brewers to allow for the use of cheaper grain and hops, so high sugar levels were a sign of poor-quality ingredients.

However, this account is described by others as a myth originating in Frederick Hackwood's *Inns, Ales and Drinking Customs of Old England* (1911). The ale-conner's oath spoke only of them tasting beer, not sitting in it. The story arises in other countries too, for example in Flanders where it was said that the tester had to sit in the puddle for an hour and the Czech Republic, where the brewer himself was made to sit in the puddle by an alderman, until it had dried. This time, if the brewer was stuck to the seat, the ale was of good quality and he was exonerated.

Another version of the story brings forward the introduction of the ale-conner by around three hundred years or more. It states correctly that a tax was imposed on beer in 1643, with two different rates, depending on whether the brew was weaker or stronger. The taster had to taste the beer to discover its strength but there is a myth yet again that the taster had to sit in the beer for 30 minutes. If he stuck, the beer was strong and if he did not, the beer was weak.

As with the first version of the story, this is not backed up by contemporary evidence. Regulations for the excise on beer, published in 1707, refer to the ale-taster's right to test the ale by tasting it, but no mention is made of sitting in it.

Another myth is that, to quote *zythophile.co.uk*, a website dedicated to lovers of beer, "the ceremony of tasting the beer is supposed to take place every 10 years at the Tiger pub on Tower Hill, where the Lord Mayor, his sheriffs and aldermen allegedly watch a member of the 'Society of Ale-Conners' test the beer's strength by sitting in a pool of beer poured onto a stool." The story arises in two books published in the 1960s.

Traditionally, in the City of London, four ale-conners are elected annually on 24 June at the same time as the sheriffs and other officials. Candidates are chosen by the liverymen in the Common Hall of the City. The livery companies were an early form of trade union. Historically, an important role such as this came with a lot of responsibility and ale-conners, bedels, sheriffs and others were required to swear an oath before being appointed. The ale-conner's oath which existed under the reign of Henry V states obscurely:

"And that you, so soon as you shall be required to taste ale of any brewer or Brewster, shall be ready to do the same; and in case that it be less good than it used to be before this cry, you, by assent of your Alderman, shall set a reasonable price thereon. . . nor when you are required to taste ale, shall [you] absent yourself without reasonable cause and true. . . So God help you and the saints."

It was decided by the Common Council in 1835 that the post was obsolete due to the introduction of standard excise duties and should be abolished upon the death or retirement of the current post holder. The Lord Mayor of the City of London decided in 1836 to bring forward the abolition of the post, but this did not happen. The post still exists in the City but has become a ceremonial role, and although it involves the wearing of solemn robes and leather breeches, its formalities are carried out in a spirit of good humour.

The current version of the job in the City of London has been described as "the best job in the world" and applications flood in annually, when the post becomes available. It comes with an undisclosed drinking budget.

Postholders are required to act as mystery shoppers, tasting the quality of beer at pubs around the capital and recording their reviews in their weekly blogs. The modern ale-conner is also tasked with hosting beer tastings and beer and food-matching classes for the general public at Old Spitalfields Market.

As reported in the *Evening Standard*, when new ale-conners were to be appointed, "a shortlist of five people will have their taste buds tested in a blind sampling at the market, in front of a panel of expert judges. . . Each then needs to give a one-minute speech on why they should get the job."

The supposed tradition of sitting in the beer does take place today and is carried out by the Corporation of London's four ale-conners but has no basis in historical fact. Today the practice of testing the ale is entirely ritualistic and is usually carried out two or three times a year when a new pub opens or a new beer is introduced. It has no legal bearing on the pub. Dr Christine Rigden was the first woman to be elected to the role in a tradition going back many centuries. The post currently comes with a nominal salary of just £10 a year.

Anchorites

ANCHORITES AND ANCHORESSES RETREATED INTO permanent seclusion in a cell, usually within the walls of a church, which would often have no door, and customarily for the rest of their lives. The word "anchorite'" is derived from the Ancient Greek "anachoretes", meaning one who retires from the world. Both men and women chose to enter into this vocation. The men were sometimes priests, but most applicants were pious lay people. It was unusual for monks and nuns to enter this way of life.

Life as an anchorite was one of the most severe ways of religious living in the Middle Ages. In some ways it was like the life of a hermit. but was more extreme than this, because it entailed permanent isolation and imprisonment. This was entered into in an elaborate ceremony in which the person being incarcerated received the last rites. After this they were considered "dead to the world". This ended with the walling up of the anchorite. Any such person who left their enclosure could be forcibly returned to it and was believed to face eternal damnation in the hereafter. Some even burned to death in their cells, when their town or village was attacked by looters or pirates.

Despite all this, there were always people who were willing to commit themselves to this vocation, which was supported by the general population as a virtuous path. Anchorites and anchoresses ate frugal meals and spent their days in contemplative prayer and in interceding on behalf of others. There is evidence to suggest that there were around 780 of them on some 600 sites in England between 1100 and 1539, when the dissolution of the monasteries was ordered by Henry VIII, which ended the practice of anchoritism in England. Most anchorite's cells have thus been destroyed but can still be seen at a few churches in England, including Chester-le-Street in Durham and at Hartlip in Kent.

There were many gradations between the role of a monk and that of an anchorite/ anchoress. Some lived their lives in complete solitude, while at the other end of the spectrum there were some who met with their fellows just for prayers or meals, and in some cases on Sundays. The strangest version of this life of solitude was that of the "Stylites" who lived for years atop high columns, from where they preached to passers-by.

Some people have been attracted to contemplative solitude either temporarily or permanently, wishing to follow in the footsteps of Jesus and John the Baptist. The earliest of these fugitives from society would retreat to be alone in the deserts of Egypt and Syria whose caves and tombs housed a great number of them.

Records of anchorites in England date back to the eleventh century, but the practice reached the height of its popularity in the thirteenth century. During this period there are records of 200 such enclosures. During the dissolution of the monasteries in the sixteenth century many anchorites and anchoresses were forcibly removed from their confinement.

Women in this vocation greatly outnumbered men. According to *compassnews.com*, "the most famous anchoress may have been Julian of Norwich who died in 1416." The publication describes Countess Jutta von Sponheim who died in 1136 as one of the other best known anchoresses. It states: "She had herself enclosed in an anchorhold beside a Benedictine abbey in Sponheim in what is now Germany. She eventually became abbess, while still walled up in her cell." She was the teacher of Hildegard of Bingen who, although never an anchoress, later took the job of abbess and became an influential member of the church, as well as a composer of church music.

By Julian's day, the incarceration of an anchorite or anchoress into their cell was formalised as a rite of the church, which was carried out by the bishop. Upon their death the windows to the anchorholds were simply sealed up.

The place of confinement was in most cases no more than 44ft 11 inches by 15 ft 1 inch (13.7 to 4.6m) in area. Some of them had several rooms to move around in and some even had their own gardens. Their cells would have included a narrow window, known as a squint, which allowed them to see into the church and in particular to see the altar. The anchorite or anchoress would also take Holy Communion through this aperture. A second window would be used to provide for their physical needs, such as food and other necessities.

A third window looked on to the outside world and allowed the anchorite or anchoress to communicate with visitors. Through this window they would give spiritual advice and counselling to the public, and so gained a reputation for wisdom. The life of an anchorite or anchoress was not just a pathway to grow closer to God, but they would become a spiritual focus for people seeking advice and guidance. Although they were physically separated from their fellow parishioners, they would be at the centre of their community, and were not necessarily lonely. Nonetheless the anchoritic life was psychologically very demanding. *Hermitary.com* describes how guides to anchoritism such as the *Ancrene Wisse*, a thirteenth century text, warned against "too much familiarity of an anchoress with a priest-confessor" and "too worldly individuals who wanted to discuss local gossip or bring gifts to the window".

Anchoresses and anchorites were not allowed to take valuables into their confinement and were barred from running a school or even from sending and receiving letters, although Jutta was not stopped from being a teacher, and it is recorded that anchorholds "served as schools, banks and post offices and even as the local newspaper".

The bishop was responsible for their care and would have to decide whether a person was suitable for this way of life. Sometimes he would put the would-be anchorite/anchoress into confinement for a probationary period, usually three years. In many cases, he would only allow people who had the financial means to support themselves to enter into this form of solitude. Sometimes, though, the bishop did provide financial assistance. Anchorites were also supported by charitable donations from all walks of life, from the King down to their fellow parishioners. Anchorites chose their path in order to assure their own salvation, while members of the public supported them in order to attain salvation for themselves.

The anchorites or anchoresses responded by giving themselves up to a life of quiet contemplation and tried to intercede for the world in prayer, but sometimes practised handicrafts to raise extra money to allow them to continue in their vocation. Many male anchorites would carry out copyist work. The anchorite life became widespread during the early Middle Ages

The *Ancrene Wisse* and another document, dating from the twelfth century, called *De Institutione Inclusarium*, gives one an idea of an anchorite's daily routine. It is estimated that the daily set of devotions set out in the *Ancrene Wisse* would take four hours. As well as completing these daily rituals, the anchorite would be required to participate in the services and carry out their own prayers and religious reading.

Whilst most anchoresses and anchorites lived many centuries ago, there are some people practising this way of life today. One of these is an Anglican called Sister Rachel who lives in a church in Peterborough, England. Her website, *www.anchorhold.co.uk,* explains how she starts her day at 4.30 a.m. with prayer which continues until 8 p.m., when she reaches the end of her day.

She told *thecompassnews.org* that "although I spend time in silence and solitude, I also generate income working in the areas of spiritual direction, leading retreats and quiet days and spiritually training." The paradox for anchoresses and anchorites is that while they withdraw from society, they also depend on it.

Animal Behaviourists

ANIMAL BEHAVIOURISTS USE THEIR EXPERTISE to understand animal behaviour in order to help both animals and humans. Some work with farmers, assisting them with livestock, and some in zoos to design suitable enclosures or observe animals in their natural habitats. Others may assist owners with their pets' behavioural problems.

The growing pet industry provides increasing opportunities for people who are interested in animal behaviour. Applied animal behaviourists can earn as much money as clinical psychologists and in many ways the job is similar, with a lot of interviewing to be done.

Understanding pets' behaviour is very much intertwined with understanding human behaviour. Family therapy plays an important role, since "people now consider pets to be part of their families", Joel Dehasse, a veterinary expert in cat and dog behaviour based in Brussels, told *Le Figaro*. Dehasse is also author of the book *Mon animal a-t-il besoin d'un psy?* (Does my pet need a psychiatrist?)

Research led by Lina Roth in Sweden suggests that stress levels in dogs mirror those of their owners. This is something that many pet owners have worked out for themselves. The research reported in the *Guardian* was based on a study of stress hormone levels in dogs' hair. This adds weight to the case that dogs empathise with their owners.

It is thought that currently around ten per cent of dogs are suffering from mental health problems, and around half of them experience mental health issues during their lifetimes. These figures are similar to those found in human beings. Sometimes during their lives, they may suffer from anxiety, depression or phobias, just as humans do. This can not only ruin their lives, but those of their owners, too.

British animal behaviourist Dr Candy d'Sa tells me it is difficult to diagnose an animal with depression or to understand its anxieties because animals cannot express exactly what they are feeling. She says both cats and dogs can suffer from Obsessive Compulsive Disorder. She adds that there is sometimes a tendency to "stereotype" the personalities of dogs and cats. She tells me the best way to deal with an agitated pet is to have a consultation to decide on a suitable action plan.

While neurosis occurs in animals, some disorders are uniquely human. Examples of animals suffering from schizophrenia are very rare and cases of psychopathology do not occur at all, according to Dehasse.

Stephen Zawistowski, a prominent US animal behaviourist psychologist, told *Monitor* magazine that "although the need for animal behaviourists is great, the field faces many challenges." This includes gaining acceptance in the scientific community and in particular the field of psychology. Zawistowski added that there has been a decline in the number of animal psychology courses in a lot of psychology departments.

Zawistowski also explained that there are relatively few opportunities for graduate students and recent graduates to find work experience as animal psychologists. "It is one thing to work with a rat in a lab," he said, "but another thing if you're in a room with a rottweiler. For people who are interested in this field, it can require persistence to get the training you need."

As in human psychiatry, the first task is to try to find a reason for the problem. It could be genetic or psychological. "Dogs cannot talk like humans, so we try to move forward relying on their various life experiences", said Dehasse.

Once this has been established, vets can prescribe medication in some cases. But their priority is behavioural therapy. They encourage a new lifestyle for the animal, one that suits both the pet and the owner. Therapy usually takes from one to six months.

"The results are even better when the owner is very much aware of the problem and when he or she puts daily efforts into helping the pet", Bruno

Legrand, a dog trainer and veterinarian in northern France, told *Le Figaro*. "But if the owner does not know the basics about the behavioural mechanisms of his or her pet's breed and about its needs, there can be serious consequences." This includes not understanding a dog's needs -- like a lot of chewing or running for miles. Ninety-five per cent of phobic or aggressive dogs will end up being abandoned or going into shelter if they do not undergo therapy.

Psychologists have been working with animals since Pavlov's well known experiment to teach dogs to salivate at the sound of a bell (1902). However, the official field of applied animal behaviour is a much more recent phenomenon, dating from the later twentieth century.

A would-be certified animal behaviourist psychologist in the US "needs a doctoral degree in biological or behavioural science with an emphasis on animal behaviour or a veterinary degree with a (component) in animal behaviour" according to *monitor.com*. Also needed are three to five years' practical experience.

Every day is different for animal behaviourists such as Andy Lattal, a West Virginia University professor. One day he might be called to decide if a dangerous dog that has attacked a person can be retrained or should be put down. On one occasion he was asked for help by a family whose pet cat refused to use its litter tray. In this case a family asked Lattal to explain this behaviour by the cat. As *Monitor* magazine describes it: "The cat had already visited a vet and been given a clean bill of health, so the problem was clearly behavioural. Lattal visited the family in their home and observed the cat's behaviour and its interactions with family members and talked to each member of the family-including two young children. Eventually the answer emerged: the family kept the cat's litter box in a closet, and the children would sometimes absent-mindedly shut the closet door". This meant that the cat could not always access the litter tray, so it learned to defecate elsewhere.

Other challenges that animal behaviourists may encounter include angry dogs and dogs with a fear of thunder, or cats that don't get on with their fellow felines. Dog psychologist Bill Gibson has explained that "it is rare for the problem to be the dog, and much more usual for the problem to be a communication issue between the owner and the dog". By understanding the way your dog thinks, you can understand its behaviour. The whole family must participate in the retraining programme, otherwise there will be no consistency and the dog will not be able to rebalance itself.

For example, a dog can make a habit of leaping up at visitors because this gets attention, which may be positive or negative. When that attention is withdrawn, the dog learns not to react to visitors in this way.

A dog with a fear of thunder can be introduced to a relatively quiet recording of thunder and given a reward for not being afraid, and then presented with recordings of gradually increasing volume until the noise matches the level of thunder itself.

Veteran animal psychologist Dr Roger Mugford told the BBC he sees an aggressive dog not as a danger but a challenge. "I enjoy making people happy" he said. "By dealing with my cases, I feel I am removing anxieties." Since 1979 Dr Mugford has run the Animal Behaviour Centre in Chertsey, Surrey, which specialises in behaviour problems in pets. The focus is on dogs but Mugford works freelance with bears, elephants and horses as well.

One of Mugford's cases was Max, an unruly one-year old border collie with an almost constant bark, whose behaviour was "unruly in a way that bordered on the dangerous", as *BBC News* described the worried owner's concerns. After interviewing the dog's owner about the animal's background, Mugford concluded that the dog was "merely misunderstood and in need of firm guidance". He then carried out behavioural exercises with the dog which confirmed his conclusions.

Mugford said his field of work, "assisting concerned pet owners whilst enjoying a flexible lifestyle," is an attractive one, but is also "full of rogues and vagabonds" taking advantage of people worried about their pets. "It isn't a regulated field" he added, advising owners to ask the vet's advice.

The job of animal behaviourist is rewarding but also challenging. Mugford said: "This job requires compassion, lots of energy, a logical mind and an ability to carry out tasks which involve an element of counselling." But he added, "some people are simply loved by animals – they have a certain magnetism and you either have it or you don't. It's not essential, but it makes the job a lot easier."

Barber Surgeons

IN MODERN TIMES BARBERS HAVE mainly one task to carry out, the cutting of hair. But from ancient history until the early part of the nineteenth century most barbers were known as barber surgeons. They would not only cut hair but carry out surgery as well. They would carry out mainly minor surgical procedures including the removal of gallstones and the setting of fractures. They also practised techniques from the letting of blood and the pulling of teeth to castrations.

Surgery was not a popular specialism with doctors, who saw it as a low profession. This was one reason why surgery was often carried out by unqualified barber surgeons. Another was that few people had the money to pay for a regular surgeon, while barber surgeons did their job on the cheap.

Because barber surgeons used a range of sharp tools, and were more affordable than doctors, they were a more popular choice for carrying out a wide variety of minor surgical tasks. They had the right tools and the right skills to carry out "paraprofessional" surgery. Mortality was high with surgery whoever practised it due to the high risk of infection and loss of blood.

As they gained experience, the barber surgeons took on apprentices who learned the trade on the job. But since feudal lords would put them to death for malpractice, they did not often attempt anything as risky as major surgery.

However, during the middle ages, they were the most common medical practitioners. As an article published by the Science Museum puts it: "In the

1500s, Henry VIII even grouped barber surgeons into guilds and forced them to distinguish themselves from regular surgeons."

The practice of the barber surgeon occurred in different cultures and on different continents as well. This included ancient China, where they were employed to castrate men. They were also found in countries where the Buddhist religion is established, in which barber surgeons would carry out procedures on the monks. Cortez discovered barber surgeons in South America. European settlers also took advantage of the surgical skills of indigenous Americans in the North American colonies. Barber surgeons also carried out tattooing and scarring in ancient Mayan civilisation. They were also known to geld animals, perform circumcisions and assist midwives.

After the fall of the Roman empire, barber surgeons became very much a part of life in a monastery. Baldness was a prerequisite for Catholic monks and was known as a "tonsure". Shaving and the letting of their blood provided a market for the barbers, who would also carry out minor surgical procedures on the monks such as the pulling of teeth.

According to the author Elizabeth Roberts, there were monks who practised as doctors, but they preferred the career of a physician, believing as most doctors did that the job of a surgeon was "dirty and beneath their dignity". In 1163 a Papal decree banned doctors from the bloodletting of monks, for theological reasons. This was left for the barbers to carry out. They also carried out all other surgical tasks as well as autopsies and embalming.

The twelfth and thirteenth centuries saw secular universities become established in Europe which would lead to a greater emphasis on the study of medicine than had previously been the case. With this came more interest in the study of surgery by academics. This led to a split between academically trained surgeons and barber surgeons which was formalised in the thirteenth century. Academically trained surgeons would thus wear long robes to denote their status while barber surgeons were expected to wear short robes to signify theirs. This led to them being referred to as "surgeons of the short robe".

These two strands of the profession co-existed uneasily over the next few centuries. They usually belonged to different guilds although in France in 1361 academics and barbers joined together as one. In England, the Barber's Company Guild, formed in 1462, merged with the Surgeon's Guild in 1540. These guilds employed inspectors to verify the work of the practitioner, as well as helping him to compete with other craftsmen who might take up the profession, by providing contracts.

Some barber surgeons were highly skilled at carrying out surgery. Ambroise Pare (1510-1590), considered the father of modern surgery, was one of these. Originally a wound dresser in Paris, he made his name with his unorthodox treatment for gunshot wounds and open injuries. He subsequently became surgeon to the French royal family.

One of the most frequent procedures carried out by the barber surgeons was the letting of blood. This was done for a number of reasons, but generally it was seen as a way of replacing bad or morbid blood with fresh healthy blood. Bleeding was carried out in various ways, including leeching and cutting a patient's vein.

Since they usually pulled teeth as well, they would often string a row of teeth in front of their shop windows to advertise this service.

Gradually, during the eighteenth century, the distinction between barbers and barber surgeons became clearer. In 1800 the College of Surgery was set up, which represented doctors who practised surgery in England. Dentistry began to emerge as a distinct specialism in the 1700s.

It was not until the 1800s that the professions of dentist, barber and surgeon became separate and distinct. As the field of medicine developed and became more effective, barber surgeons were not called upon to carry out surgery as much as they had been, and their practice gradually died out and had disappeared altogether by the 1820s.

Little sign of barbers' links with surgery and the medical profession remains today, but the still familiar red and white barber's pole originally represented the blood and bandages associated with surgery. This dates back to ancient Roman civilisation. Another example is the fact that in the UK the title "Mr" is used for surgeons instead of "Dr ,which dates back to a time when most surgeons did not have a university education. These links with the old trade remain, but surgeons must now possess a medical degree and a doctorate as well as several further years of training in surgery. Barbers are left to the profession of cutting hair.

It is difficult today to think of visiting a barber for bloodletting, tooth extraction or nail cutting, but until the nineteenth century, this had been standard practice since ancient times. The barber's shop was the precursor for a variety of occupations including surgeons, dentists, tattooists, embalmers and chiropodists as well as being a place to get one's hair cut.

Bathing Machine Proprietors

INVENTED BY BENJAMIN BEALE IN 1735, the bathing machine was soon replicated around the coast, continuing in use for the next 150 years. The first English resort to have bathing machines for general use was Scarborough, where they were introduced in 1735. In 1789, King George III had his own machine installed at Weymouth. Queen Victoria owned a bathing machine, situated at Osborne Park, her home in the Isle of Wight. Both these machines are now housed in museums at their respective sites.

In the early days of their use, bathing machines were seen as "toys of the rich" while the less well-off continued to bathe naked in less fashionable parts of the beach.

Many people believe that all bathing machines were built to a similar design. It is true that they were all wooden constructions, with small windows and steps, and many were pulled into the sea by a horse. However, machines belonging to different proprietors often differed significantly in their design. The machines designed for use by the Royal Family were much more elaborate than the basic machines used by the general public.

Although the Victorians did not invent bathing machines, the mid to late nineteenth century was certainly the period when they were most popular. It was made obligatory to use them on most main resort beaches, which meant that those who could not afford to use them were limited to paddling in the shallows.

A few machines were located at even the smallest of resorts, and since bathing was the main reason for going to the beach, high standards of accommodation were important. Hugo Westman, a resident of Birmingham, suggested providing a dressing table, but one bathing machine owner in Devon had the idea of carpeting the floor, which did not prove successful. In 1853 a Scarborough undertaker named T.W. Crosby introduced his "Patent Safety Bathing Machine" which gave ultimate privacy to the bather by allowing the water to enter the machine.

In the town of Bognor Regis in Victorian times there was a bathing machine proprietor called Mary Wheatland. She was followed by Frederick Jenkins whose business was based on the west side of the pier. His father was the owner of a fleet of bathing machines at Eastbourne. In 1886 he moved to Bognor with his wife, Margaret, and was set up in business by his father who gave him a fleet of bathing machines as a wedding present. His machines at Bognor were painted in blue and white stripes because blue was Margaret's favourite colour.

In Weymouth, in 1900, charges were 6 pence including a costume and towel, or 4d each for two sharing. There was a cheaper option, at 2 pence per person, which comprised four salons, two for men and two for women, which were supposed to be a sufficient distance apart to allow for modesty. These salons could accommodate up to 52 people in separate cabins, often reached by a rickety set of steps. In some cases, there were stewards, many of whom were female, who helped their clients down the steps and "dipped" them in the water.

Over the years these "bathing contraptions", as they were known, were damaged by the buffeting of the waves. They were replaced at Weymouth in 1923 by beach huts and the old bathing machines were broken up, except for one example which still exists today and is being refurbished to be put on display to the public.

Bathing machines were not only used Britain, but appeared in a few other countries around the globe, including the USA, New Zealand and Australia. Pictures from Australia show a shark proof fence around the front of the machines, known as a "shark guard".

However, they were more successful in northern Europe. They were particularly numerous in Boulogne, a favourite destination of British tourists. They were also popular in Belgium, especially at King Leopold's royal resort of Ostend. It was here that the machines were at their most decorative. This was where the "machine du luxe" could be found towards the end of the nineteenth century, boasting fine construction and paintwork, ornate roofs and windows engraved with scenes from the locality. Despite all the ingenuity of British bathing machine proprietors in their various constructions around the coastline, the world's most luxurious bathing machines were created by the Belgians.

On the continent, many machines were elaborately designed with great attention to detail and a steward standing on duty by the door in some cases. This made it safer for the bathers and allowed females to get changed in privacy. Sometimes canopies were used to provide a private enclosed space in which the bathers could immerse themselves.

The machines were in many cases owned by private individuals, supplementing their income from full-time work in trades such as "boatmen, fishermen, publicans and shopkeepers" (Kathryn Ferry in *Beach Huts and Bathing Machines*.) Some were owned by companies and both types of proprietors made good money out of the exercise. To raise extra cash, many proprietors used the walls of their machines as advertising hoardings. According to Kathryn Ferry: "With so many holiday makers flocking to the beaches this was a shrewd way to reach a captive audience." Soap manufacturers, such as Pears and Sunlight, were a reliable source of income for the beach hut proprietors, along with Singer sewing machines and Beecham's Pills.

The design of the machine would vary according to the specific needs of a particular beach. The beach might be flat or sloping, firm or soft, comprised of sand or pebbles and the distance to the water's edge was often markedly different.

Coastal geography, combined with local manufacturing methods, ensured that there was no standard design to bathing machines, as can be seen in the picture postcards that became available in the 1890s. It was essential that the machine was heavy enough to stand firm in the waves, despite a continual slosh of water on the underside of the floor. However, different solutions were arrived at by different proprietors in different locations.

Owners would patent their own distinctive styles to attract customers.

Paint scrapings taken from a restored Edwardian machine from Eastbourne show stripes of bright red and yellow, which leads us to believe that the fleet owned by the Hounsom family were highly colourful.

While some machines were constructed with large wheels, others were equipped with small ones, and some were winched out to sea while others were drawn by horses. Many were brightly coloured while some were plain white.

Making the machines colourful and distinctive was not just for aesthetic purposes; it made good business sense where there was more than one operator on a particular beach. For example, "in Brighton in the early 1870s there were 254 licensed public bathing machines managed by 20 proprietors." (Kathryn Ferry). Victorian and Edwardian photographs show a black and white view of the machines, whereas they were in fact a colourful, if not gaudy, feature of most British beaches. The name of the owner of a bathing machine was usually advertised on the side and each machine had a unique identification number. This avoided confusion at busy resorts where there was a multitude of them on the beach. It also made the ownership of a machine easily identifiable.

Once they had made use of the bathing machine, bathers would normally take to the waters in the early morning. There was a queuing system where as *workshops-for-schools* describes it, "those wishing to use the machines would go to a waiting room where they would pay a fee before marking their name on a slate to show their position in the queue. Whilst waiting, they could take tea, read newspapers and magazines and make small talk with other customers". Families could go together, and single people could share with those of the same sex. Sometimes the queues became disorderly when queue jumping took place.

These queues became longer with the start of the railway era. According to Kathryn Ferry: "In 1837 about 50,000 passengers travelled to Brighton by stagecoach during the year", while in 1850, with the introduction of the railway, 73,000 people travelled there in the course of one week. The purpose of people's visits had also changed. Going to the beach for health reasons, for bathing and for the sea air, was superseded by pleasure as being the main reason to make the trip.

As the tourist industry developed, along with the invention of bathing costumes and swimming becoming a popular activity, the beaches were getting crowded and people no longer wanted to wait in line for a bathing machine

Beadles

A BEADLE COULD BE AN official of the church or a university or sometimes a law enforcement officer. The term also refers to people who carry out ceremonial duties such as those appointed by the City of London livery companies. Beadles still exist today but are no longer officials of the church. The term "beadle" or "bedel" as it has also been known, is derived from the Latin word "bedelus" and the Saxon word "bydel" meaning "herald". It originally referred to an official found within Roman temples

In the Church of England, the term beadle referred to a parish constable, whilst in the Anglican church in Scotland it referred to someone who assisted the minister with the services. In England the beadle was appointed by the vestry and part of his job was to carry out the vestry's orders. In addition to these duties, he was subordinate to the church wardens and so his job included a wide variety of other responsibilities.

One of the main duties of the beadle was to ensure that the people of the parish properly observed the Sabbath. During the 1820s a group of clergymen banded together to try to "devise some way of bringing about a better observance of the Sabbath", observing that Sundays for many were a day of leisure activities such as steamboat rides and visiting public gardens or taverns instead of attending Sunday worship. The beadle also had the important job of keeping law and order in the parish and resolving disputes between neighbours.

As the historian Geri Walton puts it: "The beadle would keep order during services, served as a town crier delivering news, dispersed noisy urchins, strolled the parish, solved squabbles between parishioners, took drunks to the roundhouse (jail), and, at Christmas time, knocked on each parishioner's door and delivered the Bellman's verse." Parish beadles had a reputation for taking no rest and were among the most important people in the parish's administration. They worked seven days a week with Sundays being their busiest days, when they would marshal the young people into their places for the church service and ensure that the church wardens were seated in pews to which they were assigned, before seating themselves at the end of the aisle in a specially reserved position.

In the 1780s Sunday school was introduced, this being the one day the children were not at work earning money to support their families. It was the beadle's job to lead the procession of the pauper children of the parish from church to school.

In medieval universities such as Oxford and Cambridge the role of the beadle is maintained, with various responsibilities for management and security and providing information to visitors.

In Scotland, the medieval universities, as well as some of the newer ones, employ a ceremonial "bedelus" who is sometime given the role of head caretaker. As in England, the official role of the bedelus is to manage the administration of the university's buildings and often to provide information to visitors. Dressed in a traditional uniform, the bedelus was also responsible for carrying the mace in university processions.

Sometimes, the term beadle is used to describe uniformed security guards, such as those that patrol Burlington Arcade, an upmarket shopping mall in central London dating back to the early 1800s. As described by *atlasobscura.com,* "running from behind Bond Street to Piccadilly, it was the first shopping arcade to have a covered roof". It is a mall of exclusive shops located between Piccadilly and Old Burlington Street in Mayfair. The unique feature of the arcade is that it is patrolled by the world's oldest and smallest private police force.

Opened in 1819, the arcade is one of Britain's earliest shopping malls. It was established by George Cavendish, who later became Earl of Burlington, and designed by the architect Samuel Ware. Cavendish saw the need to protect his wealthy customers from the criminal elements prevalent in

London at the time, and with the establishment of the Metropolitan Police still ten years in the future, he decided to create a police force of his own. The arcade has a strict code of conduct enforced by the Burlington Beadles who wear a regency period uniform to this day.

Initially housing 72 shops, the 96-yard (87.8m) long, two storey, glass roofed, arcade was known for its high-end selection of "hats, hosiery, gloves, linen, shoes, jewellery, lace, walking sticks, cigars, glassware, wine and watches", according to the historian Ellen Castlelow, but the upper storeys of the buildings were in some cases occupied by prostitutes. The arcade still houses some of London's most exclusive shops including art dealers, jewellers and antique dealers, patrolled by the beadles, just as they were two centuries ago.

Several rules were established in Burlington Arcade which persist to this day. According to *Londonist.com*, these include "no humming, whistling, singing, running or even fast paced walking, riding bicycles, opening umbrellas or behaving boisterously". Some of these rules were enacted to prevent "industrious females" from signalling to pickpockets that the beadles were about. In the 1980s Paul McCartney was rebuked by a beadle who did not recognise him for whistling in the arcade. When he realised that the man in question was the famous ex-Beatle, he granted him a life-time exemption from the no whistling rule.

The only other person ever to have been exempted from this rule was an 11-year-old schoolboy who visited the arcade with his uncle when he was about six years old. He struck up a conversation with the beadles and was keen to know about the history of the arcade and the role of the beadles. He explained that he was having a tough time at school because of family problems. On hearing this, the beadles told him that if he received a good school report, he would be allowed to come back and whistle. A few years later the boy returned with his uncle who told the beadles that the boy had been working hard and had indeed received a good school report. The beadles responded by printing a document for him that gave him personal permission to whistle in the Burlington Arcade.

A beadle is also a term used to describe an official of the livery companies of the City of London, who acted, as *The Beadles of London* website describes it, as a co-ordinator between the Master, the Wardens, the Court of Assistants, and the Livery in general. Beadles also had a caretaking role for the hall where the company would hold its meetings, and responsibility for calling the Court members and or the Livery to assemble in the presence of the Master. According to *The Beadles of London* website: "They also organised the social and ceremonial functions of the Company." Historically it was a beadle's job to enforce any disciplinary measures issued by the Court. A beadle was also required to seek out suitable apprentices for the Livery Company.

They retain their role in the management of the company's property, in many cases being responsible for the upkeep of the fabric of the buildings. Beadles advise on matters of protocol and work with the Clerk to ensure the functions of the company run smoothly. They ensure the necessary regalia is in place for functions and returned to the vaults afterwards. Beadles also have responsibility for the robing of the Master and the Wardens and act as toastmasters during the proceedings. They are provided with a staff of office, often incorrectly described as a mace, officially to protect the Master and enforce discipline.

Thus, there are a variety of different roles of officials known as beadles, past and present. These range from officials of the church to law enforcement officers and ceremonial officials of the Corporation of London, where they have a history dating back 900 years, and continue in these duties to the present day.

The Bow Street Runners

LONDON'S FIRST EFFECTIVE POLICE FORCE was established and developed by Henry Fielding and his blind half-brother John, from 1748. As Don Hale puts it in *The Birth of the British Bobby -- Bow Street Runners, Scotland Yard and Victorian Crime*, "shortly after becoming established as the Chief Magistrate for the City of Westminster and Middlesex, Henry became disillusioned with the state of English law enforcement and set about introducing a series of far reaching measures to help restore law and order" in the unruly capital.

Before the Bow Street Runners were established by Henry Fielding, the Magistrate at Bow Street, the capital lacked an effective police force, as did other areas of the country. The previous system was established in the thirteenth century by Edward I. It comprised a few constables in each parish and was ineffective in preventing crime and upholding law and order. Men of a particular district would take turns of duty in the "Night Watch", but most working men could not be up all night keeping watch. Also, the job was dangerous, and according to historian Donna Hatch: "the ruffians and thugs they tried to arrest would usually fight back".

According to Don Hale: "The Fielding brothers were highly critical of the Parish Constables and particularly of the night watchmen", describing them as ineffective and pointing out the limitations to their power. Henry claimed constables were "disorganised and inefficient", suggesting that criminals had little to fear from them.

The constables, also known as "'thief takers", were infamous for their misbehaviour. They would act as intermediaries between victims and their attackers, for example arranging payment for the return of stolen goods and blackmailing offenders with the prospect of prosecution. Some, such as a man named Jonathan Wild, would even stage robberies to get the reward.

Henry Fielding was a lawyer and satirist whose work was published in many of the newspapers and magazines of his day. It is claimed that the success of his first novel, *Joseph Andrews*, written around 1737, allowed him to avoid incarceration in the debtors' prison. His best-known novel is the classic *Tom Jones*. As Hale records: "He made numerous satirical attacks on the Government of the day and particularly on Prime Minister Walpole, and when the politician was finally deposed from office, the new Government rewarded Fielding's efforts with a prominent position as Justice of the Peace for the City of Westminster." In addition to this, "the following year he took responsibility for the county of Middlesex, presiding over the court at Bow Street".

In 1750, Henry went about creating the Bow Street Runners who were, according to Donna Hatch, "an elite fighting force of highly trained and disciplined young men". These men were trained in basic forensics, how to conduct investigations and in how to question witnesses and victims. They also carried handcuffs.

During the first few years there were only six men employed as Runners, but the number later increased, and a mounted patrol was even set up outside the capital to protect the travelling public against highwaymen.

Although the Runners usually operated in the London area, some even ventured as far as the Scottish borders to apprehend their suspects.

To allow a greater area of jurisdiction for the force, Henry was made a commissioner of the peace in Surrey, Kent and Essex as well as Bow Street and Westminster. This made it easier for the Runners to operate in these counties, because they did not have to seek authority from other magistrates there. Although Sir Henry received £200 from the government for the project, this was soon spent. This meant that for a time they were paid mostly by reward from the victim of a crime or someone with an interest in solving the case. Later this was supplemented by a weekly salary of just one guinea.

According to Hale: "His unique thief takers. . . became the first detective force and were known as the 'Robin Redbreasts', for wearing distinctive scarlet waistcoats." Over time the Bow Street Runners gained a formidable reputation for carrying out investigations and apprehending suspects. They could also issue writs.

For Henry Fielding, publicity was an important tool in his investigations and rewards, lost and found notices and successful prosecutions appeared in newspapers of the time. The Runners encouraged the public to provide as much information as possible. His policing methods required the extensive use of informants and he communicated with these through advertisements and pamphlets published by the Bow Street office. He found that turnpike gatekeepers and publicans were particularly useful sources of information.

He called for important changes to the legal system and brought in the help of his brother John to assist him with his onerous task. John Fielding, known as "the blind beak", also went on to become Chief Magistrate for Middlesex and the City of Westminster after his brother died. According to Hale, "Newspapers claimed that he could even recognise the voices of up to 3,000 criminals who had appeared before him." Although many of these were fast tracked to the gallows, he tackled social problems and took measures to promote the rehabilitation of first-time offenders.

John also encouraged victims of crime to report the incidents and it was he who established the country's first specialised detective force. In so doing he was responsible for the setting up of an extensive criminal records system and shared this information with police forces that were developing in other localities. "In addition, John Fielding addressed the threat of highway robberies, by setting up a team of 10 mounted officers employed to patrol suburban areas." (Hale). "This proved so successful and the threat from highwaymen so much diminished that the patrol was disbanded", adds Hale. This led, of course, to the return of the highwaymen.

While undertaking his duties at Bow Street and Westminster, he developed a central collection point for evidence of serious crimes that took place up and down the country. John Fielding was knighted in 1761 as a reward for his efforts in creating the country's first effective police force.

By the late eighteenth century, the Runners had become full time policemen and often put in many years of service. It has been argued that their detailed testimonies in court have changed the nature of criminal trials. Until this time, although a defendant was strictly speaking innocent until proved guilty, a guilty verdict was usually a foregone conclusion. Some people took advantage of this for the purposes of revenge in matters that were not relevant to the courts.

Since the constables were paid by reward, there was a bias towards them providing their services to the better off members of society. Nevertheless, Fielding's system eradicated much of the gang violence that had previously been prevalent in London.

In 1792, the Middlesex Justices Act set up similar forces to the Bow Street Runners across London. So, the principle of using paid officers to detect crimes and apprehend offenders in the capital was established long before the creation of the Metropolitan Police in 1829. But affluent areas had been policed much more thoroughly than less well-off areas of the capital.

During the early years of the nineteenth century the policing role in London of the Bow Street Runners declined, as new forms of law enforcement took their place. This meant that they earned less money, since they received fewer rewards. Their position at the forefront of London's police force gradually ebbed away. By the early 1820s only around 10 per cent of cases brought before the Old Bailey were instigated by the Runners. From 1815 the Runners were mainly tasked with assisting prosecutors based outside London, where their skills and experience were considered beneficial.

After the introduction of the Metropolitan Police, the role of the Bow Street Runners in policing London was further diminished, and they were gradually incorporated into the new force. The Home Office believed that cost of the Runners was too high, and this meant that the funds made available to them declined sharply in the 1830s.

In 1834 a parliamentary committee recommended that the Runners should be incorporated into the Metropolitan Police as soon as possible. However, this did not immediately take effect. In 1839 another parliamentary committee came to the same conclusion and expanded upon its findings. The recommendations of these committees were enacted into law in 1839. The Runners were finally redundant.

Cartography

WHEN A MAP BECOMES FAMOUS it is usually due to it being particularly beautiful, revolutionary or historically significant. Cartography is both a science and an art and involves making maps or geographical representations and images on a given scale. They can help us to understand topography and other features of the landscape depending on the type of map.

Early forms of cartography were maps inscribed on clay tablets or cave walls. As time went on maps were eventually drawn on paper, depicting places that explorers had discovered. Technological advances such as the invention of the compass, the telescope, the sextant, the quadrant and the printing press made maps more accurate and easier to produce. Present day maps represent a wide range of information and "the advent of technology such as Geographic Information Systems (GIS) allows maps to be made relatively easily with the use of computers" (*thoughtco.com*).

Some of the earliest known maps date to as far back as 16,500 BC, but represent the night sky rather than the surface of the earth. Some early cave paintings portray distinct features such as hills and mountains and are believed to have been made for the purposes of navigation in the areas they depict, for example hunting grounds.

Maps on clay tablets from ancient Babylonia have been discovered and appear to use complex surveying techniques. In addition to illustrating topographical information such as depictions of hills and valleys, they included labelled features. An important example of this type of map is The

Babylonian World Map. The ancient Egyptians created maps on papyrus, but since this is such a fragile material, few examples survive.

Among those created by the ancient Greeks, Anaximander's map of the known world makes him one of the earliest cartographers. Other map makers included Herodotus and the Greco-Roman mathematician, geographer and astrologer Ptolemy. The maps they created were based observations made by explorers and mathematical calculations. Though of limited usefulness for the purposes of navigation, these maps provide an insight into the way cartographers, explorers and geographers of the time understood the world known to them. The concepts of longitude and latitude were introduced by Ptolemy and have influenced cartography ever since. His maps have never been found, but his detailed descriptions of them allowed medieval scholars to recreate them in 1300 AD.

Many of the ancient Greek maps placed Greece at the centre of the world surrounded by an ocean, while others depicted the known world as two continents, namely Asia and Europe. This idea was based on the works of Homer and other Greek writers of the time. In fact, many early Greek cartographers believed the Earth was spherical with a central fire at its core. Attempts by ancient Greek cartographers to measure the circumference of the Earth brought about a huge boost to cartographical science. Their maps date back to the fourth century BC and were inscribed on wooden blocks.

Other early maps include examples from the Romans who made maps for practical purposes including military, economic and administrative needs, required in order to control their empire. Maps from ancient China show various features such as the Jialing River as well as roads which were mapped for economic purposes. Map making gradually developed in ancient China with an early example of a map with a grid system dating from the Sui Dynasty in 605. A large 29 ft 10 inches by 32 ft 10 inches (9.1m by 10m) map was inscribed in 801 during the Tang Dynasty to depict China and its Central Asian colonies. This map used a highly accurate grid system.

During the middle ages, Islamic scholars continued the traditions of map making of earlier cultures, mostly following Ptolemy's methods, but also making use of the discoveries of explorers and merchants since that time. The *Tabula Rogeriana* was created in the twelfth century for Roger II of

Sicily by the Islamic scholar al-Idrisi. It is not only a map but also a comprehensively researched geographical text that describes ethnic and cultural groups and gives socio-economic information as well as natural features and other characteristics of the area covered by the map. As *gislounge.com*, a mapmakers' website, puts it, "al-Idrisi drew on his extensive travels, interviews with explorers, and draftsmen paid to travel and map their routes". This map shows the earth as spherical, and broken into seventy rectangular sections, each of which is described meticulously in the *Tabula.*

In medieval Europe, decorative, symbolic maps began to emerge, such as the Hereford *Mappa Mundi,* which is still kept in Hereford Cathedral. It is circular, highly coloured, and detailed and places Jerusalem at the centre of the world. During the 1300s, Mappa Mundi was a term used for maps of the world in general, derived from the Latin 'Mappa' and 'Mundi' meaning of the world.

An Italian monk called Fra Mauro created a world map in 1450, known as the *Fra Mauro Map*, which is considered "one of the world's finest surviving pieces of medieval cartography" (*gislounge.com*). The map is "round, about two metres in diameter, painted on vellum and stretched on a wooden frame", the website adds. It depicts Europe, Africa and Asia, which was the entire known world to Europeans at the time. It differs significantly from Ptolemy's maps in that the south is orientated at the top. This is because Fra Mauro believed Ptolemy's cartography to be outdated and inaccurate, as much less of the world had been discovered at the time of its inscription.

Cartography continued to develop in Europe during the "age of exploration" as merchants and explorers mapped the areas of the world that they had discovered. They also charted the oceans for the purposes of navigation.

The rise of printing, new instruments of measurement and surveying in the sixteenth century led to cartographers becoming men of great influence in the world's most powerful nations. This happened as economic expansion, colonisation and the quest for military superiority brought about the need for accurate maps to allow countries to control as much of the world as they could. The first map of the Americas was created in the early 1500s by the Spanish cartographer and explorer Juan de la Cosa who accompanied Christopher Columbus on his voyages of discovery. In addition to the Americas he produced maps which detailed Africa and Eurasia.

The first scientific world map, known as the *Padron Real*, was designed in 1527 by Portuguese cartographer Diogo Ribeiro. This was a significant development because it accurately depicted the coasts of Central and South America as well as coverage of the Pacific Ocean.

A big advance in cartographical science came about in 1569 with the publication of the first in a series of maps by Gerardus Mercator, which resulted in what is known as the Mercator Projection. This map is significant because it is the first one that attempts to make a spherical world look 'right' on a flat surface. Lines of latitude and longitude are rendered useless on a flat map, so Mercator kept his lines straight by distorting the areas close to the poles. Because Mercator's maps used straight lines, they made it easier for ships' navigators to chart a course, despite the issue of the distortion.

This became a standard world map and was mathematically based with greater accuracy than anything that had preceded it. Later in this century and during the 1600s and 1700s more areas of the world that were discovered by Europeans were mapped for the first time, with increasing accuracy.

After the advent of the industrial revolution, world travel became more widespread for recreational as well as trading purposes. Later, during the nineteenth century, a network of railways was established across the globe, which made travel more accessible and affordable to the general public, as well as much faster. Maps showing the latest additions to the railway network were produced diligently by cartographers, with decorative features almost disappearing to be replaced by purely factual information.

As new technology continues to improve, map-making improves with it. Modern day cartographers are well versed in the use of computers, image-processing, spatial analysis and software. As Geographic Information System technology has become global, GIS analysts and specialists have become the experts of cartographical science. GPS tracking, originally available only to the US military, and the globalisation of data have greatly boosted the science of cartography today.

Technology is now developing so rapidly that it is difficult to predict what the next innovations in cartography will be. Nonetheless, computer technology has revolutionised cartography and has ushered in a new epoch in map making.

Coracle Fishing

CORACLES WERE SMALL BOATS USED mainly on rivers and lochs. Bigger versions were used at sea. Coracle fishing is an ancient tradition in Britain, dating from pre-Roman times. These are one of the earliest types of boats ever constructed. This kind of fishing continues to be practised today in Wales on the rivers Teifi, Taf and Tywi. There is also a long history of coracle use in other cultures, for example Vietnam, Tibet and India and Iraq.

Although each coracle is unique in its design, they can be described as oval, rather like a walnut shell with a frame of willow rods interwoven like baskets, tied with willow bark. Animal skins were traditionally used to construct the outer layer and made waterproof by the application of a thin layer of tar, while today tarred calico or canvas and sometimes fibreglass are used instead. The boat has a flat bottom so that the weight of the craft and its load is spread evenly and so as to allow for going out on shallow water such as rivers. A plank serves as the seat in the vessel. Coracles were built by those who used them, and the techniques were passed on from generation to generation and within the community.

Each coracle is designed specifically for the river conditions where it is to be used. Generally, each river has its own design, but this is not always the case. Coracles on the River Teifi, for example, are designed to float on shallow rapids, which are frequently encountered on this river in the summer. Coracles on the Tywi are designed to be wider and deeper, in order to cope with tidal waters with no rapids.

The coracle is rowed using a broad-bladed paddle, which again differs in its own specific design for different rivers. This is propelled in a figure of eight motion. The boat is designed to float on the water rather than in it, making it difficult to manoeuvre for all except the expert oarsman.

The paddle is positioned at the front of the boat with the paddler facing the direction of travel. Coracles are light and portable. The fisherman would often carry the craft on his shoulders, with a leather strap across his chest, for five to ten miles before drifting downstream. Teifi coracles are carried over the head rather than on the shoulders like those in other places, with the paddle hooked under the seat. Nets are carried on top of the boat.

Coracles are generally used when the fish are travelling back from the sea to spawn, mostly at night. Their most effective feature is that, when navigated by a skilled person, they hardly disturb the water and the fish at all. The craft can be easily manoeuvred with one arm, while the fisherman controls his net with the other. In the South Wales rivers, two coracles are used co-operatively to manage one net. This is stretched between the two coracles and drawn downstream. When a fish is caught, each of the two coraclers lifts their end of the net and draws the two boats together. The fish is then retrieved and stunned using a wooden implement known as a priest, so called because it is said to administer the last rites.

Dylan Jones, Secretary of the Coracle Society tells me: "The coracle is the oldest type of boat still in use on British rivers." He adds that it is not clear when and where it originated but it is thought to date from as far back as the Bronze Age. He says it was certainly hundreds of years old when the Romans arrived and was used by the Celts at the time of Julius Caesar.

Whilst mostly used for fishing, coracles have also been used for military purposes. Having seen coracles for himself, Caesar ordered his troops to make boats of the same design for use in his military campaign in Spain in 49 BC. This is the earliest documented use of coracles although they are mentioned in the Welsh *Mabinogion*, which refers to them as "corygeu".

Today the Coracle Society seeks to maintain the tradition of coracle fishing and to encourage newcomers to coracle making and use. They offer coracle building classes as a tourist activity which are currently on offer at the Greenwood Trust in Ironbridge where coracles can occasionally be seen on the River Severn.

Traditionally, coracles were used on several British rivers including the River Spey where the boats were heavier and stronger than in other places, which improved manoeuvrability of the vessel in this fast-flowing river. A coracle that is believed to be more than 300 years old is displayed in the Elgin Museum in Scotland. According to *wovencommunities.org*: "It was found in the roof of a farm building at the mouth of the River Spey and was donated to the museum at some point between 1859 and 1868".

Coracles on the River Spey in the eighteenth century were not used for fishing but instead for transporting timber downriver to the sea. This was a distance of about 30 miles (48.3 km). The timber was felled nearby in the Scots pine forests of the Strath Spey. It was carried on rafts attached to the coracle by a horsehair rope. This was carried in one hand by the boatman while he paddled the boat with his other arm. Once they had reached the sea the men got out and returned to their point of embarkation carrying the coracles on their backs, in order to get the next raft. This work was both dangerous and skilful, because the Spey is one of Britain's fastest running rivers. This also demonstrates how resilient the craft were to the conditions on the river.

Coracles were traditionally used for fishing on the River Dee and as flexible, lightweight and flat-bottomed boats they were suitable for this river with its strong currents and a shallow, rocky bed. Two men would fish together at night-time with a net stretched between their two coracles. Over the centuries, as Liverpool Maritime Museum describes, "at times several hundred coracle fishermen worked on the River Dee and in 1882 they caught almost 11,000 salmon along with over 600 trout". Fishing in this way was prohibited there in 1920 to protect fish stocks and to raise more revenue from sports fishing.

According to Ceredigion County Council: "About 100 years ago, there were 300 coracles in use on the River Teifi alone". Due to the efficiency of this method of fishing, regulations were put in place to protect fish stocks, and it is strictly regulated.

Coracles have a long tradition of use on the River Teifi and this is one of the few places where they are still in use today. Coracle fisherman Mark Dellar tells me the best place to see coracle fishing is at Cligerran on the

Teifi. He says, "it is a good place to watch and follow" since "there are multiple pairs fishing in the area". This can be done during the fishing season which runs from 1 March to 31 July, on weekdays. Dellar adds that they generally meet there before dark "as the first pair hits the water at dark". The Teifi coracles were also used for livestock rescue and sheep dipping.

There is a tradition of coracle races on the river which goes back a long way. Until relatively recently a race was held on Boxing Day on a twelve mile stretch between Llechryd and Cardigan bridges. At the time of writing an annual regatta is still held in Cligerran as part of the annual River Festival held there since 1950.

Malcolm Rees is one of the few people still using coracles on the river Tywi to catch salmon and trout. He owns several fibreglass coracles and still manufactures them using traditional materials and methods. Coracles are generally about 5ft 4 inches (1.63 m) long, 3 feet 3 inches (1m) wide and 14 inches (36.6 cm) deep. Rees comes from a family of coracle builders and fishermen with a history dating back three hundred years. He is passing on his skills to a nephew and cousins, who live nearby. However, it is no longer possible to make a living from this activity, although catches are sold to local restaurants. There are currently only a handful of pairs of fishermen active on each of the Tywi and Taf and Teifi rivers.

Historically, coracle fishing has been a men only tradition partly because the strap of the boat goes across the chest when carried on one's back which makes it difficult for women to carry. However, there are currently some female coracle fishers who also go out in the boats, according to Dellar.

From its origins thousands of years ago, coracle use has been practised more or less continually to the present day. Wales is now the only place where coracle fishing still regularly takes place in the traditional way, but it is currently threatened by licensing restrictions and is confined to the Teifi, Taf and Tywi rivers.

Cryptozoology

SINCE HUMAN BEINGS FIRST WALKED the planet, they have told each other stories about strange, mythical creatures but it is only for a little over a century that modern cryptozoology has existed.

A manuscript entitled *The Great Sea Serpent* was published in 1892 by Dutch zoologist Anthonie Cornelis Oudemans. Oudemans suggested that sightings of a large sea serpent were actually those of a giant, elongated seal. However, despite Oudemans' reputation as a respected scientist and Director of the Dutch Royal Zoological Gardens, few people took his book seriously, and the existence of the serpent has not been established.

Another major figure in the history of cryptozoology was Bernard Heuvelmans, who in 1955 published his book *On the Track of Unknown Animals* which has led him to become known as "the father of cryptozoology". He described many animals from around the world that were rumoured to exist, but whose existence had not been proven. His work encouraged many people to go in search of these "cryptids".

Today cryptozoology is covered extensively by television shows like Finding Bigfoot and Beast Hunter, which is shown on the National Geographic Channel and a number of other programmes. With all the coverage that Big Foot gets, it is perhaps surprising that no clear evidence of his existence has been found to date. Despite these limited opportunities for cryptozoologists in the media it is generally not possible to make any money from cryptozoology.

It is seen by most scientists as a pseudo-science and has no degree programmes or indeed any qualifications at all. It is also extremely difficult to gain the respect of other researchers. There are plenty of monster hunters out there who give cryptozoology a bad name. A serious biologist or zoologist who practises cryptozoology is likely to lose all credibility. The progress of cryptozoology is slow and it is difficult but not impossible to detect new species. A researcher might spend a lifetime in a fruitless search for an animal for which only anecdotal evidence exists.

There are some well-known examples of cryptids of whom there is much anecdotal evidence but no hard facts. One of these animals, of which there have been most sightings, is Big Foot, also known as Sasquatch in the Pacific North West. The animal has not only been spotted in the USA, but also in the Himalayas where it is known as the Yeti. Some cryptozoologists have suggested that has evolved from the extinct great ape Gigantopithecus Blacki. There have been sightings all over Canada and the USA, some of which date back to Native American times, so if it does exist this would be one of the easier cryptids to spot.

Another famous cryptid is the Loch Ness Monster which is a creature fabled to exist in the deep water of the huge lake Loch Ness in Scotland. This leads by waterways to the sea, causing speculation that "Nessie" could be a sea creature, or one that travels to and from the sea. Some cryptozoologists believe Nessie is a Plesiosaur, an aquatic reptile that most scientists believe is extinct.

The Orange Pendek is another ape or primitive hominoid, spotted in the forests of Sumatra whose name is a translation of "short person" in Indonesia. It is possible that they are more closely related to modern humans. The discovery of the bones of a species of small, prehistoric humans known as Homo Floresiensis on the Indonesian island of Flores led to suggestions that the Pendek was a relative of these, hidden in the jungle and rarely spotted.

The Mapinguari is a creature that may be a species of giant sloth, thought to have been extinct for thousands of years. Nonetheless, it is reputed to menace people living in South American jungles "with a mouth on its stomach, backward facing feet, huge claws and a horrible stench" (*gaia.com*).

A massive shark over fifty feet in length stalked the world oceans thousands of years ago and fed on marine mammals such as whales. This is the Megalodon, which was the largest carnivorous animal in the world. According to modern science, it is long extinct, but some people believe it still exists, deep in the oceans. Strange creatures once thought to be extinct have been rediscovered before, and much of the world's oceans remains unexplored.

Some people even argue that dinosaurs still exist. The Mokele Mbembe is a mysterious creature known to the people of the African Congo. According to *gaia.com*, it is described as "having the body of an elephant, with a long neck and a small head". Several other dinosaur-like creatures have been spotted in and around the Congo River basin. This has led some researchers to suggest that there may be an isolated population of dinosaurs in the area. This theory goes against our knowledge of the history of the planet, but eye-witness accounts do exist.

Nevertheless, thousands of new species are discovered every year. At the time of writing, around 1.8 million species have so far been identified. In his article, *What is Cryptozoology?*, David McConaghay states that "over the last half century, scientific estimates of the total number of living species have ranged from between three and 100 million." The most recent survey estimates that there are nearly nine million, of which 6.5 million live on land and 2.2 million in the oceans. Given the size of unexplored habitats such as rainforests and the depths of the oceans, it is likely that this is a conservative estimate. If only 1.8 million out of a total of nine million animal species have been discovered, this leaves another 7.2 million species yet to be identified.

According to Loren Coleman, Director of the International Cryptozoology Museum in Portland, Maine, USA, cryptozoology "literally means the study of hidden or unknown animals". It is, as David McConaghay puts it, "an actual science based on rumour and hear-say", which tries to legitimise local legends and myths, making it different from mainstream science. These stories would be easy to dismiss were it not for the growing category of formerly mythical creatures being proved real.

One of the best-known examples of such animals is the Pongo which in

African folklore was described as a wild man of the jungle. With the appearance of being half man, half monkey, he was feared for his violent temperament and his seemingly magical powers, as well as his rumoured taste for human flesh.

It was in 1847 that a shocked scientific community learned that the pongo was a real animal. It is now one of the world's best-known animals, the gorilla. Gorillas are vegetarian and did not deserve the fearsome reputation with which they had been tainted. So, the animal was real, but its sinister notoriety was not. Nonetheless, the name "gorilla" is derived from the Arabic word for "ghoul".

Another cryptid proved to exist is the Coelacanth, which is known to have existed in pre-history but was thought to have become extinct about 65 million years ago. This changed in 1938 when one of these fish turned up in a South African market.

After it had been identified as a coelacanth it was preserved as a taxidermic specimen, but the scientific establishment tried to deny that it was in fact the creature that they had declared long extinct. Some people attempted to claim that it was a grouper, even though it did not resemble this fish. In 1952 a second coelacanth was discovered alive, and since then many of them have been captured and two sub-species identified. Thus, despite fierce resistance from the scientific community, the existence of the coelacanth is now an indisputable fact. It is classified as a cryptid since despite its known existence in prehistory, from the fossil record, it was considered no longer to exist.

Humankind has always had a fascination with the unknown. It is likely that there will always be unconfirmed stories of mythical creatures which will continue to provide a place for cryptozoology.

Daguerreotype Photography

THE APPEARANCE OF A DAGUERREOTYPE is unlike that of any other form of photography. The image is on a mirror-like surface normally kept under glass where light striking the polished silver plate illuminates an eerie and delicate silvery image which is extremely sharp. The image appears to be floating in space and has a realistic quality, especially when it is well exposed, which is unique to the medium. The image will appear either positive or negative depending on the angle at which it is viewed and how it is lit. A daguerreotype has a level of detail and resolution which is greater than that of the digital photographs of today.

It requires a good deal of skill to create this type of photograph. The artist would polish a sheet of silver-plated copper until it had a mirror like surface. Initially this was done manually but buffing machinery soon became available. The plate would be treated with bromide and iodine fumes to make its surface light sensitive. It was then exposed in a camera for the necessary time, which varied according to how well the subject was lit. This was done by removing the lens cap and creating an invisible latent image on the plate. Next, the latent image was revealed by fuming the plate for a few minutes with mercury vapour. This was well known to be toxic, but the daguerreotypists were willing to take the risk. The plate would then be treated with chemicals to remove its sensitivity to light. This process was known as fixing. After this was done the plate was rinsed and dried and the resulting delicate and easily damaged image was placed under glass.

Gilding was often applied to the resulting image by a process introduced by Hippolyte Fizeau in 1840. This gave a warmer tone to the picture and made the image less delicate and prone to damage.

Daguerreotype photography was invented by Louis Daguerre (1787-1851) a French artist and inventor, who developed the first practical photographic process in 1837 after eleven years of experiments. Daguerre did not invent photography, for which credit must be given to Joseph N. Niepce, (1805-68), but he did create the first practical photographic process.

This method produced a single photo, a positive which could not be reproduced, except by lithography or engraving. This came to be known as a Daguerreotype. The picture was a mirror image which could only be viewed properly in a certain light.

As the online article "History of Photography" puts it: "Daguerre strolled about the streets of Paris with a heavy camera and bulky equipment, made his daguerreotypes on boulevards, arousing interest in people, but did not explain the essence of his method." He tried to set up a corporation by public subscription and when this failed, he endeavoured to sell the rights for it for a quarter of a million francs. This also came to nothing, so he tried to attract the interest of scientists in the daguerreotype. One of these was physicist D. F. Arago who passed on the details of the invention to the French Academy and encouraged the French government to buy the patent.

Arago persuaded Daguerre to accept a pension from the French Government for his efforts. Niepce was also rewarded with a pension. Daguerre was also awarded the Legion d'Honneur and was granted a patent in England.

He went to great efforts to promote his invention and arranged demonstrations for artists and scientists. Together with a relative, A. Giroud, he began manufacturing daguerreotype cameras for sale. They shared the profits equally, but Daguerre granted half of his takings to Niepce. The invention did indeed gain widespread popularity and within a year the instructions had been translated into many languages. Daguerre and his photographic invention became famous worldwide.

Other scientists, artists and enthusiasts improved upon Daguerre's method, reducing exposure time and inserting a prism into the camera so that it would no longer reproduce a mirror image. By 1841 a smaller camera became available, which was ten times lighter than Daguerre's. There were also some improvements to the durability of the image.

Even with more sensitive plates and quicker exposure times, without the use of studio lighting an exposure on a bright day took several seconds. In dull weather the sitter had to remain motionless for considerably longer. The lighting was controlled using blinds and screens to make it more diffuse.

Among the prominent practitioners of the craft were the amateur Jules Itier (1802-1877), a Frenchman who travelled to China to create a photographic record of the country between 1843 and 1846, and Johann Baptist Isenring (1796-1860), a Swiss national who specialised in landscape photography. Among those working in the UK were Antoine Claudet (1797-1867), a student of Daguerre whose work can be found in the National Portrait Gallery's collection, and Thomas Richard Williams (1824-1871). Examples of his work are in the collection of the Science Museum in London. He was famed for his stereoscopic daguerreotypes and his pictures of the royal family taken in the 1850s and 60s.

The daguerreotype method quickly became popular in the USA where it was practised by, amongst others, portrait photographer James Presley Ball (1825-1904) and Albert Easterly (1809-1882). Easterly was one of the best-known daguerreotypists in the American mid-west during the 1850s. He took landscape and cityscape photographs as well as portraits. Another prominent US daguerreotypist was Augustus Washington a black photographer and campaigner against slavery. John Adams Whipple (1822-1891) specialised in astronomical photography and night-time pictures.

When he heard about the invention of the daguerreotype William Henry Fox-Talbot pressed ahead with his invention, known as the Calotype, which was "the first process of its kind that resulted in a negative paper image that could be reproduced into many positive images", according to United Photographic Artists' Gallery. He achieved success in 1840 and took out a patent on the process in England in the following year. The resulting positive image was less sharp than a daguerreotype but afforded the pictures a moody, artistic quality. It was an easier process which was more popular with amateurs than the daguerreotype and which encouraged them to take tourist photos and proto-snap shots.

Nevertheless, the daguerreotype was highly successful within a few years of its introduction, and many portrait studios were set up in European and US cities. Portraiture was now available to most people, not just to the wealthy elite as painted portraits were. Commercial photography also gained a foothold, but the main use of the process was for portrait photography.

Tradesmen without any artistic skills were able to successfully run portrait studios. Photographic portraiture quickly became widespread, particularly on the East Coast of the USA. The calotype was never as popular as the daguerreotype but made photography practical for amateurs. Soon, a lot of people were creating photographic images, albeit often mediocre ones, particularly in the case of the calotype. This met with the disapproval of some prominent art critics, who believed that photography was "cheapening art".

Towards the end of the twenty-year period when these two media were popular, some photographers introduced new visual techniques, compositional tools and lighting effects. This gave the medium a more creative and artistic value, leading to the acceptance of photography as an art. By 1860 these two processes had been superseded by glass negatives and the albumen print which paved the way for modern photography. Without it, the world as we know it would not have been possible.

Dendrochronology

WE CAN LEARN MUCH FROM the study of tree ring growth, which is known as "dendrochronology". This includes the age of the tree, past climatic conditions and freak weather events. Due to the wide range of scientific disciplines that dendrochronologists are involved in there are no specific degree courses in the subject. Most people who participate in the study of tree ring growth are either tree scientists (dendrologists), climate science specialists or archaeologists and chemists. Although there are no degree courses, there are training programmes in the study of forest management and conservation which include dendrochronology. Dendrochronology is also used by medieval studies graduates, classicists, and historians who need to be able to date some of the materials which they deal with in the course of their research. A bachelor's degree in any of the above disciplines is usually sufficient for the study of dendrochronology.

The process of tree ring dating was invented around 1900 by the American scientist Andrew Douglass who was interested in climate change. He argued that tree ring data could be used to provide a record of past climate, going back far beyond what had previously been possible. His theory was confirmed, and the more trees we study, the greater the historical record, which allows us to understand how the climate has changed over the centuries.

The study of tree ring growth is based on the fact that every season, a tree ring is typically set down in the trunk of the tree. As *EnvironmentalScience.org* puts it: "We can see this on any tree stump, a series of concentric rings, circling the heart of the wood and fanning out towards the edge." The outer rings obviously record the newest growth and the inner ones record the earlier life of the tree.

Some trees are more reliable than others for the dating of tree rings. Oak is the one that provides the most accurate information, with no known cases of missing annual tree ring data. Alder and pine are well known for being less reliable and sometimes miss out yearly rings. Along with this these, trees sometimes have two rings for one growth season. Birch and willow are too erratic in their growth cycle to be used successfully. Since the Industrial Revolution, some growth records have become more erratic, as climate change gathers pace.

Since in unusual conditions, trees may miss a ring, or produce more than one ring a year, dendrochronology is not as simple as it might seem. Nonetheless the general rule is that there is one ring produced for each annual growing season. The width of each ring varies from year to year which indicates different rates of growth. For example, growth in a hedgerow that does not have competition from larger trees will occur more quickly than a woodland tree which will grow more slowly until it has become tall enough to reach the forest canopy. Weather events such as storms and infestations by pests and diseases all affect the growth of a particular tree ring. Some of these are uniform, but others are thicker, lighter or darker. These differences represent the different weather conditions that occur from year to year.

The weather during the growing season affects all trees of the same species over a wide geographical area in the same way. Thus, the ring record should be the same for all trees of the same species in the same region, which means that, after a great deal of study, the dendrochronologist is able to determine a mean pattern of growth or chronology.

The practice of dendrochronology in general is based on this information. In some geographical areas weather patterns make this relatively simple. In the hot and arid conditions of the south-western USA a wet year means a wide ring will be set down while a dry year will produce a narrow ring. Although it is possible to learn something by studying just one tree, when hundreds and thousands of records are compared, the potential to learn from the tree rings is enormous. It is an accurate and reliable way of gaining useful data for the purposes of, amongst other disciplines, environmental science and archaeology.

The complex climate in the UK was considered a problem for the study of tree rings, until the late twentieth century. More recently a number of dendrochronologists have been studying tree rings in the UK from trees that have lived for hundreds of years and records that date back millennia in the case of archaeological studies. Tree ring records from most parts of the UK have now been established. They have created a master chronology of trees that have lived for hundreds of years in particular areas of the country.

It was not until the 1970s that most archaeologists saw the value of dendrochronology to their own field of study, even though Douglass had himself used the study of tree rings to date Indigenous American artefacts and monuments, the age of which had previously been unknown. Such organic archaeological material allows us to "create a chronological record against which artefacts can be dated" (*EnvironmentalScience.org*). These will often be examples from prehistoric civilisations.

Until the 1980s dating archaeological sites was often impossible. Before this time there was very little chronological information for the prehistoric era in England. This was because it is only rarely that organic material is found preserved from these times. One such example is the Sweet Track in the Somerset levels which is the oldest known preserved artificial footpath in the world. When this was discovered it gave researchers the ability to date the track and its surrounding settlements to around 3806 BC. As *EnvironmentalScience.org* puts it "From this point dendrochronology became a fundamental tool in the dating of archaeological remains."

Dendrochronology is also a useful tool in dating oak timbers used in the construction of buildings, by studying the end grain of timber beams. The outermost ring relates to the year in which the tree was felled. This may help to estimate the age of a building, but sometimes timbers were recycled from other constructions and dendrochronologists can only establish the year a tree was felled. However, it was unusual to use a large batch of recycled timbers on one site, so by matching several timbers from a building to the same age, a better understanding of the age of the construction can be gained.

Normally they take a core from the wood by drilling a hole in it or if it is no longer in use, complete slices of the timber may be taken. This is a far more destructive process but gives a much clearer indication of the chronology. In order to establish this chronology, other timbers from the same area need to be studied. Most dendrochronologists prefer at least fifty rings to study from one tree. Unless there are sufficient tree rings to study in a timber, and the result can be compared with several other examples, the dendrochronologist will not be able to determine the age of the timber.

With dendrochronology in the field of environmental science, in the fight against climate change, we study the past to try to predict the future. Dendrochronology plays an essential part in our understanding of our regional and global paleoclimate. There have been great advances in this field of study over the past twenty years. With climate change that has occurred since the onset of the industrial revolution, the focus is on human activity, but dendrochronology tells us about previous climate change which has occurred naturally. It can tell us what effects of past rises in carbon dioxide levels have had on the environment, which helps us to predict the effects human-made carbon emissions will have in the future.

Trees are commonplace in many places across the globe. They provide the oxygen that all animal life needs to breathe. They date back approximately 380 million years and live in a huge range of climatic conditions, from the arid to the tropical, to the temperate regions of the planet. They are ubiquitous in their use for aesthetic purposes in parks and gardens. Trees can be found in all shapes and sizes, from saplings found in most countries to the giant redwoods of North America. Although often taken for granted, they offer a valuable insight into history.

Dry Stone Walling

THE BUILDING OF DRY STONE WALLS has been carried out for thousands of years, dating back to the Neolithic era. The walls are called dry stone because there is no mortar or cement between them. This allows the structure to settle naturally and makes it resistant to frost damage. People who have built these walls over the centuries have made an important contribution to the rich heritage and tradition of the British Isles.

Prehistoric walls that still exist include those in the Neolithic village of Skara Brae on the island of Orkney dating from around 3000 BC. Other examples include the brochs built by the Celts, and examples can be found as experienced dry stone waller Scott Winship puts it, “around the world from Egypt, Japan and South America to the turf walls of Iceland”. The craftsmen who built them were highly skilled and it is said that the stones are packed so tightly together that one could not fit a razor blade between them.

In the UK, the Celts built the walls to keep livestock together and to set out the boundaries of crop fields as they moved from being hunter gatherers to become farmers. Stone circles were sometimes built as well, for ceremonial or religious purposes, such as the ones at Avebury and of course Stonehenge.

In Viking and Anglo-Saxon times there was a resurgence of wall building. Some existing walls can be dated back to the time the Vikings first settled in England, but many can only be identified from remains left in the ground.

Wall building became prevalent again in the UK during the fourteenth and fifteenth centuries and continued until the eighteenth century, due to the enforcement of land enclosures which meant the landowners took over what had previously been common land. Most of the dry stone walls that exist today were built during the eighteenth and nineteenth centuries for land enclosures.

Dry stone walls can be found across the UK marking out a network of field boundaries over various types of terrain. They are not only historically and culturally significant but continue to serve as livestock boundaries. They reflect the geological differences across the UK. Most are built where trees and hedges do not grow due to the harsh climate or thin soils, and where rock is to be found near the surface. The majority of them can be found in the higher altitudes of northern and western Britain.

Historically, walls have usually been crafted using local materials. These are generally preferred, as it would be too costly to import materials from further afield. This means that there are regional variations in the type of stone used. For example, slate was used in the Lake District and gritstones found in the Pennines were used there.

Dry stone walls are sustainable structures, assembled with very few tools. They are long lasting and have little need for maintenance. The craft of building them is highly skilled and involves techniques passed down over the centuries.

Livestock can take advantage of walls to seek shelter in bad weather and they also provide a haven for plants and small animals, including insects, and serve as wildlife corridors which allow them to move about safely.

Today there are around 70,000 miles (112,650 km) of dry stone walling in existence in England alone. The majority of these are in need of repair. A government report in 2007 drew attention the threat to landscape heritage if these walls are lost. It also highlighted the fact that only 13 per cent of them were in a good state of repair, with 17 per cent in an advanced state of disrepair, and a further 50 per cent in the early stages of decay.

According to the Built Landscape Heritage Education & Training Project, "in recent years many dry-stone walls have fallen into disrepair due to the decline in upland farm incomes and the lack of grants to subsidise the cost of repair work." Without well maintained walls, the problem of keeping livestock together makes hill farming more difficult and less cost effective. The dereliction of the UK's dry stone walls must be halted if this useful and historical feature of the landscape is to survive.

The Dry-Stone Walling Association of Great Britain, founded in 1968, aims to encourage learning of the skills required for this ancient craft. The DSWA offers accredited certification in the practice so that the craftsmen and women of today can maintain and repair the walls throughout the country. The DSWA is particularly active in the West Pennines, where it works with other conservation organisations to halt the decline of the walls. Bursary trainees are mentored by qualified wallers and along with volunteers they work together on projects to restore the walls, enhancing the landscape for tourists and maintaining historical features.

HRH The Prince of Wales takes a particular interest in the subject and helps promote the work of the DSWA. The Prince's Countryside Fund, in association with *Lancashire Life* magazine, has provided funding for the training of young people in the craft around the country.

Linda Clarkson, training and education co-ordinator with the DSWA told *Lancashire Life*: "There is a skills gap which has opened up in the countryside." She added that the grandfathers of today's farmers would have had dry stone walling skills, but during the 1970s and 80s contractors were brought in instead and so the farmers did not pass on their skills in wall building to the next generation. Since grants are no longer available for the maintenance of dry stone walls, farmers today do not have the finances or the time to invest in the upkeep of these walls, and this is why so many of them are in a state of disrepair.

Clarkson said: "Our aim is to engage with young people and make them want to have a try at dry stone walling." They are then encouraged to develop their skills and gain a qualification. "We not only fire up the enthusiasm of young people so that they can go out and do the work on their own farms but also see it develop as another source of income", explained Clarkson. Although wallers can earn money from contract work on local farms, the big growth area for their craft is in landscape gardening, in which they can earn much more money.

Only a few women have qualified with the DSWA as advanced stone wallers, and one of these is Lydia Noble. According to *Lancashire Life*: "She passed her Advanced Walling Certificate in 2013 and she went to her local show in Penrith where she came second in the Cumbria Walling Grand Prix. Noble went on to win the overall championship later in the season." Young farmers and rural workers like Noble are helped with funding by the Prince's Countryside Fund in DSWA courses across the country.

As Noble told *Lancashire Life*, despite the often harsh weather conditions, dry stone walling "can be quite therapeutic" because it "allows you to create something physical that has a purpose as well as preserving habitats for small animals and maintaining the country's historic features".

Enumerators

THE FIRST CENSUS IN ENGLAND and Wales took place in 1801 and has been followed up with another one every ten years since this date. However, before 1841 the names of all the occupants at a particular address were not recorded. From this time onwards, censuses were administered in districts based on those used for the registrations of births deaths and marriages. These often matched the parish boundaries, but this was not always the case.

The 1841 census has some limitations when compared to later ones. Exact ages and relationships within the household are not given, and place of birth is simply listed as in the county of residence or outside of it. Nonetheless it was the first "modern" census, organised at a national level, with about 35,000 enumerators taking details as quickly as possible to avoid discrepancies as people moved from place to place. The census districts were sub-divided into enumeration districts which were made up of about 200 households or an area in which the work of the census could be carried out in one day. An enumerator was responsible for each of these.

By 1851, 40 per cent of workers were employed in manufacturing. Service workers, including domestic servants, retail workers and professional people comprised 25 per cent of the workforce. The relatively small percentage of people employed in agricultural work reflects the fact that during the Victorian period, Britain was rapidly becoming an industrialised economy. From census to census, many people would change their occupations and jobs such as handloom weaving went into decline, to be replaced by factory and engineering work. Increasingly as people took on new occupations, they moved from the countryside to the towns and cities of Victorian England.

As the population grew rapidly during the nineteenth century, thousands more enumerators were appointed. According to *BBC History*, "the labour force reached 16.4 million by 1901, about seventy-five per cent above the 1851 figure. Over the same period, the total population increased by about 78 per cent, reaching thirty-seven million."

The enumerator would in many cases have to visit slum tenements in which many different households lived together and one room would often house an entire family. Some enumerators in rural districts would have to travel a wide area of scattered households or communities.

For the 1851 census, John Pearson, a farmer who lived near Chorley in Lancashire, was appointed to the job of enumerator. He was paid 26 shillings for the work. He had to familiarise himself with the householders' forms and the enumerators' books in which he would record all the details given by the householder. Pearson was required to acquaint himself thoroughly with the district in which he would be working, including the total number of households he would have to visit. Then, over the week before census day, which fell on the 8 April, he had to deliver the schedules to each household. The following day he would return to each address to collect the information, helping the illiterate to answer the questions, checking the details with the householder and making any necessary amendments. After visiting 159 households comprising 840 people, his work was done.

In taking down these details, according to official regulations, an enumerator was required to be "intelligent, trustworthy, active, able to write well, and have some knowledge of arithmetic". He was also supposed to be "temperate, orderly and respectable, conduct himself in strict propriety and civility in the discharge of his duties". By the time of the 1891 census, women were allowed to become enumerators. The work was demanding, and some enumerators did complain about the long hours and paucity of reward.

A householder's schedule was delivered to every household along with instructions on how it should be completed. The head of household was required by law to complete the form on census day, recording also the names of persons sleeping in the house that night. Night workers who would be returning in the morning to sleep also needed to be recorded. In the case of households with over one hundred occupants such as schools, hospitals, workhouses and other such institutions, a different schedule was provided.

From 1851 to the early twentieth century the census was always held on a Sunday in March or April. This was because on a Sunday evening most people would be at home, and during these two months most agricultural labourers were not yet working away from home. Like John Pearson, the enumerator would return the following day and collect the completed forms.

From 1841 to 1901, once all the data had been collected, the enumerator would enter it into the Census Enumerators Book (CEB). The returns and the CEB details were cross checked by the district registrar before being sent to the Census Office at the General Register Office in London, which was later renamed the Office of Population Censuses and Surveys. They were double checked by this office and the householders' schedules were destroyed. Using the CEBs, the Census Office extrapolated and published a range of population data. It should be remembered that where the householders' schedules have been destroyed, this information was now a secondary source and may have been reproduced a number of times by different people, which means that mistakes were bound to occur.

Over time, a few of the CEBs have been lost. It is also possible that despite the thoroughness of the exercise, some individuals have been omitted from the records. As Phil George of *historyhouse.co.uk* puts it, these records represent only "a snapshot of a household and its occupants" which may not reflect the usual composition of the household.

During the nineteenth century in particular, illiteracy, language barriers and dialect were problems often encountered by enumerators in some areas, for example in London's East End, where many people did not speak English. Not all enumerators were as literate as they were supposed to be and would replicate misspellings of names given by the householder, such as Emerly (Emily) and Auther (Arthur).

Sometimes the definition of a member of the household as a boarder or a lodger was interpreted by the enumerator according to their own ideas of how these should be recorded as were the relationships of family members.

The record of place of birth could be specific, for example stating the parish in which a person was born, or they could give only a vague indication, as by simply stating the county of birth. Sometimes the enumerator would not record this information accurately, but census returns over a period of time will give a more reliable account.

People who worked in a number of different trades, or did seasonal work, could only be recorded by enumerator as having one standardised occupation. It is thought that the occupations of many part-time workers and people who worked at home were not reported in the census. Several thousand women's suffrage protestors boycotted the 1911 census, which seriously affected the accuracy of the records.

Individual house numbers were a rarity in villages and in urban areas "many street numbers did not exist or changed over the decades because of the rapid growth and development of Victorian towns and cities" (Philip George).

Despite such omissions and discrepancies in the census data, the information that they provide gives a valuable insight into historical population, working lives, family relationships and society in general. They are also a vital tool for discovering family history, used alongside various other sources, such as records of births, deaths and marriages.

Food Styling

FOOD STYLISTS NEED TO COMBINE culinary skills with a basic understanding of chemistry, in order to present food at its most appetising. Food styling is also an art that requires a good sense of composition.

Food stylists prepare and arrange food for photography, and the resulting pictures are used in cookbooks, magazines, product packaging and advertisements. Styling for advertising purposes can be notoriously difficult. As food stylist Jennifer Joyce told the BBC, it also tends to use a little more trickery than other presentations, for example dyes, paints and lipstick are used to add colour to a dish. Many food stylists have a passion for the creativity of work on food magazines or cookbooks. They tend to seek out and buy the most attractive of foods, often visiting several stores before finding what they are looking for.

In the past inedible products were used in food styling, which led the end results to be quite fake-looking. Today, stylists like to make their presentations as realistic as possible, although some on occasion will, for example, replace ice cream with mashed potato, because of the problem of melting.

It is essential that they understand the techniques, tools and principles involved in their craft and have some knowledge of the media in which their creations will be appearing. They also need to be creative, have good attention to detail and be skilled in the instruction of photographers and assistants. Natural lighting, focus and colour clashes between the food and the props all need to be considered. This presents the food to its best potential. Food stylists usually cook the food themselves before arranging it for the camera.

Since most magazines and TV shows are usually produced months before they appear, this can mean, for example, a food stylist cooking a Christmas dinner in July. In fact, many stylists spend the summer months creating Christmas dishes.

The first task is a trip to the supermarket or more specialist shops such as butchers, greengrocers and fishmongers. The stylist will get to know where obscure ingredients can be obtained. The task of cooking the food may involve several dishes, with accompaniments, to be made ready on the day of the shoot. Obviously, this can be time-consuming and means a lot of hard work. Jennifer Joyce told the BBC: "I have a big toolbox I take with me to the studios, containing anything I might need." This includes a potato masher, a zester, a thermometer and a peeler. She added: "I also take a separate bag containing bigger items like a blender, a hand mixer, pastry cutters, blow torch and an assortment of all types of wooden skewers."

Mari Williams, who is also a food stylist, explained one of the most painstaking jobs she has done. This was for a client who sells rice. For this shoot she had to individually select grains of a certain size and colour and arrange them using a pair of tweezers. She told the BBC: "It was painfully slow and used all my reserves of patience."

Some stylists also photograph the food themselves. When styling and photographing food it is essential to work as quickly as possible so that the food stays fresh. "Shiny foods lose their lustre, oils and sauces soak into cooked meats and such foods as herbs and lettuce will wilt away quickly", as Nicole S. Young, author of *Food Photography: From Snapshots to Great Shots* records. It is important to check regularly that the food is still fresh, replacing or touching up anything that has become limp or lifeless. For this reason, it is a good idea to have extra servings on hand to replace any that no longer look their best.

Sometimes a stylist may use stand-ins for the food while they are preparing the shot, so that the food will be fresh when it is placed in front of the camera. These can be anything from a burger bun to any item with a similar shape and tonal qualities to the food presentation.

In the past the food would often wait for hours in the studio while the photographer adjusted cameras and lighting. Today in the age of digital photography, all this has changed and the job is much simpler and less time consuming. Stylists need to have some knowledge of photography, even if they do not take the pictures themselves. This will give them an idea of how the food will look in the photograph.

According to Jennifer Joyce, food styling "is a very competitive field" and "it is pretty vital to have a qualification from a respected cooking school like Leiths School of Food and Wine or Le Cordon Bleu." Aspiring stylists also sometimes take courses in Art and Design. Even observing a food stylist at work is a good way to gain experience. After that one must start out as an unpaid assistant for about six months and next if successful move on to a paid assistant's job. Then it can take a year to achieve a styling job for oneself, having learned the skills the job requires. However, a talent for the job is also needed.

Another stylist, Katie Marshall, tells me that one of her favourite recent clients was Cadbury. She adds: "I had to make amazingly decadent hot chocolates to be advertised on social media. When I was part way through the shoot it struck me that the chubby little child inside me would be very proud." She also enjoyed working for Coca-Cola and PepsiCo where the imagery would be used across Europe, which she describes as "quite exciting".

Marshall is freelance and is employed for a day or a few days at a time. She loves the variety in her job, saying: "Every week is different, and this can be scary as well as exciting. I get to work with different photographers and creatives all the time." She tells me that "it also means that I get to work in different locations across London, helping to create beautiful imagery with cool teams of people."

Marshall explains that she generally cooks the food herself. "Sometimes I have an assistant and we cook the food together, and I'll be the one to do the final tweaks before it is photographed. At other times we're working with prepared products (like supermarket sandwiches) so it is our job to do some tweaking to make it look its best."

Concerning "fake food", she says that "mostly with editorial photographing (for cookbooks and magazines), it is easiest to use real food! You want the food to look delicious, but realistic – and slight imperfections (which are unavoidable) make the recipes look more achievable for home cooks, which is the whole point of our jobs. We want readers to see a finished product of the recipe it is printed or posted next to and believe that they can and want to recreate it at home."

When I asked about her typical working day, she explained that "every day is different, but normally I'll turn up at a photography studio with all my ingredients at about 8.30am to start cooking. I'll come up with a schedule for the day based on the order I can cook the dishes and we'll work our way through six to eight recipes." Marshall works with a prop stylist who will have selected props and backgrounds which will make the food look at its best, which she then uses to plate up the food. Since the shots are normally taken in natural light, length of the day in winter restricts the hours they can work. "Sometimes it's a bit of a race against time", she says, but one of the perks of this job is "getting to try lots of tasty food!"

Professional Foraging

THE HARVESTING OF "WILD FOOD" that grows prolifically in the UK such as leaves, nuts, fruit and fungi, has become a new industry which supplies food to many restaurants and has stimulated increasing public interest in foraging.

Different ingredients are available in different months and foragers harvest around 200 of these annually. Some of these grow in abundance, such as hazelnuts and blackberries, while others are harder to track down, such as certain types of mushrooms and elm or lime leaves. Restaurateurs will pay up to £40 for 2 lb 3 oz (1kg) of morel mushrooms and £50 for the same quantity wood sorrel, which has a sharp lemony tang.

The Forestry Commission estimates that in Scotland alone, wild harvesting is worth around £21 million a year, and is taking care to encourage foragers to use these resources responsibly and where necessary seek the landowner's permission. As well as seeking out food some foragers look for certain types of mosses and lichens which act as natural remedies.

Foraging is no longer just a cottage industry and fruit and vegetable wholesaler Fresh Direct, which supplies stores such as Harrods, as well as top restaurants and high street cafés, has expanded its foraging operations from Scotland to England. We are in the midst of a "wild food" revival but world-famous chefs such as Hugh Fearnley-Whittingstall have long espoused the value of locally sourced foods that occur naturally in our forests and countryside.

Wross Lawrence, a professional forager who works on the East Sussex coastline, told journalist Lizzie Rivera: "Seven years ago people would look at me weirdly and ask what I was doing. Now people stop me and ask what ingredient I'm picking." Lawrence works full time March to October supplying the organic food delivery company Abel & Cole.

The current popularity of foraged food has led to fears of exploitation of natural resources, such as the reports of illegal gangs in Epping Forest reported in the *Guardian* in 2014. As the fashion for foraging increases, it may be necessary to employ local stewards to police the activity.

If everyone took up the activity, the impact on our woodlands would be disastrous. Warnings have already been issued in the New Forest about the depletion of the fauna and flora which foragers are supposed to be honouring. Too many foragers are not good for the natural habitat. In Bristol this failure to respect foraging led to legislation being put forward to prohibit the public from "uprooting plants or taking any part of them in parks and public spaces" (*sustainablefoodtrust.org*).

Foraging is a popular activity in Sweden with the law allowing "freedom to roam". There is a level of trust and respect for the natural habitat there which is less prevalent in Britain. Properly managed foraging is important to the preservation of the ecosystem and can provide opportunities for sustainable agriculture as well as contributing to the health and nutrition of the public.

The public's increasing choice of using foraged foods to cook is encouraged by their growing interest in where their food is sourced. There is no food that is more organic and sustainable, when properly managed. Forest foods are good for one's health, for example for digestion and heartburn. Lawrence has led a group of children with liver disease in foraging activities to alleviate their condition, as part of their Duke of Edinburgh Award. "It's what the body was used to eating for thousands of years before farming", said Wross. "There's nutrients in foraged food that you don't get in cultivated food".

Only a few chefs know how to use foraged foods to good effect. One of these is Rene Redzepi at Norma restaurant in Copenhagen. Others include David Everitt-Matthias of "Le Champignon Sauvage" in Cheltenham and Matthew Pennington, co-founder of the Bristol restaurant "The Ethicurean".

He aims to put at least one foraged garnish on every meal in order to raise the profile of foraged foods with the public. As Pennington put it to Rivera, "Guests commonly say 'I had no idea you could eat that – it's all over my garden and I thought it was weeds'.' "

The modern British cuisine served at the Ethicurean is often compared to that of the Scandinavian style, where foraging is widespread. Foraged food cooked in the Scandinavian way greatly influences its equivalent in British cuisine. If Redzepi gets his way, we will all be eating foraged insects a well as plants. He founded the Danish not-for-profit Nordic Food Lab which has published a book espousing the nutritional and economic advantages of eating forest insects. This includes advice on how to build a termite trap and digging for grubs. The eating of insects has not yet caught on in a big way in the UK.

Forageable plants are usually sourced from the countryside, but they are also available in big cities if one knows where to look and what to search for. One person who does is John "the poacher" Cook, who forages across London to provide wild foods to "chefs, chocolate, cheese and gin makers", according to Rivera. He prefers to use a barter system such as wild garlic for cheese. "Foraging becomes a compulsion" he says. "I've been on the top deck of a bus, seen a mushroom ring on an estate and just had to get off."

The ever-increasing popularity of foraging has led many people to go out into woodlands across the UK in search items from wood sorrel for Michelin-starred chefs to spruce needles used to flavour hand-made chocolates. Professional forager Yun Hider runs his own business, the Mountain Food Company, sourcing wild foods in Pembrokeshire, South Wales. As he tells journalist Alex McRae: "I work for chefs as their hands in the forest. I go to estuaries, hedgerows and mountainsides, and track down the finer wild vegetables such as wood sorrel and sea beet and deliver them to restaurants either in person or by courier." He said that he usually works alone but sometimes he employs one or two helpers.

Hider said what he likes most about the job is connecting with nature. "People have been gathering wild food for thousands of years, and I love keeping that tradition alive", he explained. "Working with Michelin-starred chefs is great too." The downsides of the job include working in bad weather and freezing cold conditions in winter when he can only go out for 30 minutes at a time. He said that there is not a great deal of money to be made in foraging, so he supplements his income by working part-time as a tree surgeon.

He explained that the professional forager needs to have an understanding of botany, including some knowledge of Latin plant names. The ability to identify plants and forage safely is a must, since there are plenty of poisonous plants out there. "When you think you've identified an edible plant, get a second opinion from someone you trust, who's prepared to eat it" said Hider.

With the number of foragers on the increase, the Association of Foragers is an international organisation set up in 2015 to support sensible practice in this fast-growing economy. This includes courses run by foraging educators to promote responsible foraging and advice on how to take care of the habitat in which the forageable foods can be found. These include foraged plants, seaweeds and fungi. According to its website, all members of the association "have signed up to a common code of conduct and actively promote sustainable, safe and mindful foraging". The association works with statutory authorities to make sure that foraging is recognised and catered for in land use policy, arguing that studies prove that people who go out foraging develop a respect for the natural world, and become good guardians and advocates for Nature.

Funambulism

FUNAMBULISM, ALSO KNOWN AS TIGHTROPE walking, is a science as well as an art and is the skill of walking along a thin wire or rope. It has a long history dating back to ancient Greek and Roman times and is a traditional circus act. The word is derived from the French funambule and the Latin funambulus (from the words funis, meaning rope and ambulare meaning to walk). In ancient Greece it was considered more of an entertainment than a sporting event and was not included in the Olympic Games.

Funambulism continued during the dark ages. In fifth century France funambulists were forbidden to perform near churches, and since this was where most fairs were held, there was effectively a ban on funambulism. However, by the 1300s funambulism was in favour again and at the extravagant coronation of Queen Isabeau in 1389 in Paris, a funambulist clutching candles walked a rope stretching "from the spires of the City's cathedral to the tallest house in the city", says American historian Barbara Tuchman. In 1547, at the coronation of Edward VI in Westminster, a funambulism display also took place. In mid-sixteenth century Venice a new event was established for the opening of the annual carnival, known as "Svolo del Turco", where a Turkish acrobat walked an inclined rope "between the bell tower of St Mark's Church and a boat docked at the Piazzetta", according to the online magazine *Atlas Obscura.*

In England, during the 1600s, funambulism came to be associated with disreputable people such as pickpockets, streetwalkers and con men. In late eighteenth century France, says *Atlas Obscura*, "one of the most well-known funambulists was Madame Saqui", who "performed many times for Napoleon Bonaparte, often walking a rope with exploding fireworks all around her". She also performed at Vauxhall Gardens in London and ran her own circus for several years. Saqui is mentioned in William Makepeace Thackeray's *Vanity Fair* and performed into her 70s.

During the nineteenth century, funambulism was increasingly associated with indoor circus acts. The first non-white circus proprietor in Victorian Britain was Pablo Fanque, who began his career doing equestrian stunts and rope walking. His own circus, in which he continued to perform, was called 'Pablo Fanque's Circus Royal'. It rapidly became popular and continued to draw large crowds for thirty years. Fanque's circus toured the country over this period and included many benefit events. One of these was for the circus performer William Kite, which is referred to by the Beatles in their song Being for the Benefit of Mr William Kite.

As the nineteenth century progressed, the stunt every tight rope walker wanted to do was to walk across the Niagara Falls. The first person to achieve this feat was Jean Francois Gravelet, known as the Great Blondin, who according to present day circus performer Chris Bullzini, is probably the best known "household name" in funambulism. In his time, he was so famous that his name was used as a generic term for a rope walker for many years, Bullzini tells me. He first crossed the Falls in 1859, stopping on the way to drink beer that he had hauled up from a boat. He is reported to have returned to the Falls many times carrying out ever more extreme stunts, allegedly stopping to cook an omelette mid-way and even achieving such incredible feats as crossing the Falls riding a bicycle, going across blindfolded or on stilts and on another occasion carrying his manager on his back. Following in his footsteps was William Leonard Hunt, known as the Great Farini, one of Europe's best-known funambulists in his day who is reported to have wire walked the Niagara Falls with a washing machine strapped to his back in 1860. As he walked along the wire, he stopped to wash several handkerchiefs which he later gave to admiring onlookers.

The first woman to achieve the stunt of crossing the Falls on a tightrope was Maria Spelterini, who had performed circus acts since the age of three. She did this for the first time in 1876 and repeated the epic journey many times, and according to *Atlas Obscura* she did so "once with her wrists and ankles manacled, once with a paper bag over her head and once with peach baskets on her feet".

Funambulists continued to carry out ever more amazing feats. Ivy Baldwin made history by walking across Eldorado Canyon several times, even as late as her 88th birthday in 1948. Philippe Petit crossed a wire strung between the two towers of the World Trade Centre in 1974, a quarter of a mile (400 m) above ground. According to Bullzini, this beat the altitude record a high wire walk at the time, although higher altitudes have been achieved crossing between two air balloons. In 1989 Petit walked an inclined wire attached to the second level of the Eiffel Tower. In 2010, Chinese funambulist Adili Wuxor, known as China's "Prince of the Tightrope", set a world record by walking a rope for nearly two hundred hours across the Bird's Nest Olympic Stadium in Beijing, which took him 60 days. In 2013 he achieved a wire-walk of 1,640 ft (500 metres) across the Pearl River in Guangdong, at an altitude of 328 ft (100 metres), stopping to sit down, dance and stand on one leg on his way.

In 2014 Nik Wallenda, who came from a family of funambulists going back seven generations, known as the Flying Wallenda circus family, walked for 94 feet (28.6 m) along a wire between two Chicago skyscrapers, while blindfolded, at a height of 600 feet (183 m). This epic feat was filmed, but with a ten second delay in case he fell, which thankfully he did not, and the stunt landed him a Guinness Word Record to add to the nine that he already held. Some of his forebears were not so lucky. On several occasions they walked a wire in a seven-person chair pyramid, a trick which they first performed in 1947. They did this without a safety net and there were fatalities on a few occasions, the worst in 1962 when three of their number fell to their deaths.

While most people would not even dream of crossing such dizzying heights on a wire, unless it was in a nightmare, an experienced funambulist can accomplish this with an understanding of the physics of the human body. "Posture is the absolute most important thing" Sonja Harpstead, a tightrope instructor at Circus Warehouse in New York City told the Smithsonian Institute. She explained that "the key to balancing on a tightrope is to lower the body's centre of gravity towards the wire". The performance is less risky if the artist's body mass is closer to the wire.

Harpstead added that most amateurs try to accomplish this by leaning forwards. Although this may achieve the desired aim of lowering one's mass, it also makes one lose one's bearings. "Then it's hello pavement." said Harpstead. She instructs her students instead to stand up straight while lowering the hips and bending the knees. This will help them bring their centre of gravity closer to the wire without losing their sense of posture and balance.

Funambulists need to be aware that the wire tends to rotate. Each time the person steps forward, the wire may spin underfoot, which can easily make the walker lose their balance. Only an experienced tightrope walker can safely avoid this, by using a technique called "rotational inertia", which means that they position their body to fight against the wire's tendency to rotate. Many funambulists find that it helps to carry a balancing pole. Phillipe Petit carried a pole that was twenty-six-foot (7.9 m) long when he walked a wire strung between the top of the two towers of the World Trade Centre.

As Petit put it: "After a few steps I knew I was in my element" although he knew the wire was not well rigged (there had been serious problems with the rigging the night before). He added: "It was safe enough for me to carry on. And then, very slowly as I walked, I was overwhelmed by a sense of easiness, a sense of simplicity." But the idea walking high above the ground, along a thin wire without a safety net, is such a stressful endeavour that it is unthinkable for all but a few daredevils such as Petit.

Golf Ball Diving

ABOUT ONE BILLION GOLF BALLS are lost on golf courses around the world every year. Sometimes they end up in a rabbit hole or a thorny bush. What golfers hate the most, however, is when the ball drops into a water hazard. For golf ball divers, though, this is an opportunity of which they take full advantage. One hundred million golf balls are retrieved and resold annually, at a huge discount, which has made golf ball diving into a multi-million-pound industry. There is a lot of secrecy and competition in the industry and no one wants anyone else to know which particular courses contain the largest number of balls.

Since water features are more common on US golf courses than they are in the UK, American golfers lose around three times as many balls as their British counterparts, around 30 in a year for each golfer.

The quantities of balls involved makes golf ball diving a lucrative business and provides a return for golf course owners whereby golfers can buy the retrieved balls at around one third of the price of a new ball. Less energy and raw materials are needed than in manufacturing new golf balls, which is good for the environment. However, golf ball manufacturers do not like the business of recycling balls. They argue that although the balls may look as good as new once they have been cleaned and recoated, in fact the aerodynamic qualities of the ball are damaged by being submerged for months under water.

The tension between golf ball manufacturers and used ball sellers reached its worst when Acushnet, the owner of the Titleist brand, sued a recycling company for reapplying the Titleist logo. They lost their case as the court said that the refurbishment company, Nitro Leisure Products, had made it sufficiently clear that the balls were recycled. This case was a landmark victory for the golf ball refurbishment industry, allowing them to continue retrieving and rebranding submerged golf balls on a large scale.

In order to collect balls from water hazards, a diver simply dons a scuba costume, makes sure his/her oxygen tank is working, submerges into the water and finds the lost balls. After remaining in the water for about an hour "a golf ball collector could emerge with a couple of bags, containing anywhere between 500-2000 golf balls" according to *myjobhub.com*. These bags weigh up to 30kg each. Once the balls have been thoroughly cleaned, they are ready for sorting. They are graded according to their state of repair, with damaged ones being discarded. They are then sorted according to brand. Some of the less damaged balls are refurbished which can mean removing parts of the outer cover or repainting them to make them look as good as new. (This can include re-inscribing the manufacturer's name).

An hour's work in the water can earn the diver around $100. When a golf ball lands in a water hazard "it's like a deposit into the bank account", golf ball diver Forest W.S. Rothchild told *Alert Diver* magazine. He added: "It's a unique way to make money doing my favourite thing: diving." It has been reported that golf ball divers can earn between $50,000 and $100,000 per year. Rothchild added that golfers hit more than 10,000 balls into a single water hazard each season. As he put it: "There are some truly horrendous golfers out there".

Divers must first liaise with golf courses to ensure that all the relevant contracts are in place and the necessary preparations have been made to allow them to do their work. If the diver works for a retrieval company, he/she will be paid per ball and the company will then sell them on to a large organisation which will resell them in bulk to a variety of golf courses. Divers who work independently miss out the middleman and sell directly to the golf courses. A typical independent diver who has contracts with 10-20 golf courses will collect around 3,000 balls a day in a five-hour shift.

A diver working for a retrieval company must co-ordinate with their area dive manager to ensure that they do not conflict with other divers or climb into a water hazard that another diver has just visited. The professional diver will usually have to visit a number of courses which may require much travel between the various sites in a given time. For an independent diver, days on the road will necessitate accommodation costs. This way of working is tough for a person with a family. Once the diver has got to the course and collected the balls, cleaned and refurbished them, the next task is to store and transport them which can involve a lot of red tape and preparation.

Retrieval companies use trained divers who have qualified from golf ball diving courses. It is not difficult to become a golf ball diver -- an entry-level diving certificate should suffice -- but to actually carry out the role is a different matter altogether. Experienced divers used to crystal clear, tropical waters often won't last five minutes in the murky, cold, and muddy water hazards of a golf course. They can see virtually nothing and have to feel their way around the depths of the water to retrieve the lost golf balls. In the trade this is known as "braille diving". While they are doing this, they have to carry their bags, which when full of golf balls are a great weight.

Divers have discovered a miscellany of items ranging from a BMW car to a telephone booth. The plant and animal life that lives in the water features can be dangerous even for the trained diver. In many cases in the southern US, lakes contain snakes and alligators, as well as snapping turtles, who will be hostile to the presence of a diver in their territory! As Brett Parker, a diver at Dallas Athletic Club's Golf Club put it, when asked by a course employee if he had seen any snakes recently: "It's not a matter of whether I've seen them; it's only a question of how many and how big." Parker also reported in *scubadiving.com* that he had been bitten by snakes three times already. As well as the alligators and the snakes there are other hazards such as pesticides, broken glass and even fishing lines with which divers are known to have got caught up, which has on occasions caused them to drown. As *scubadiving.com* puts it: "Golf ball divers treat death with the same casual interest that rock climbers do." They all know or know about people who have died doing the job.

Illegal divers are universally despised by the professionals who call them Nighthawks, Captain Midnights and Night Hunters. "Most of them are criminals and thieves", Mike Gerstner, the owner of a retrieval company, told *scubadiving.com*. As one of the poachers themselves put it: "They pretty much give you a slap on the wrist for it."

This was not the case for John Collinson who in 2001 emerged from a water hazard at a golf course in Leicester, UK, with 1,158 "lakeballs" as they are known in this country. He was arrested and sentenced to six months imprisonment, but his case was covered on television and many Brits thought he had been unfairly treated for such a minor offence. Even the prime minister, Tony Blair, intervened and Collinson was released early. However, since his arrest created so much publicity, it has proved something of a cash cow for him with many offers of legitimate golf ball diving work coming in.

While divers working illegally generally do their work at night, legitimate divers are more often active during daylight hours, being careful not to damage the course and being mindful of golfers. However, the golfers do not always reciprocate as a US golf ball diver told *Alert Diver*: "One time a golfer almost hit me with his club. He'd seen bubbles coming close to the shore and when I emerged from the water, he was poised to hit me with his nine iron. He thought I might be a 'gator or a giant snapping turtle."

In the early 2000s a lot of money was being made by people searching for golf balls underwater. Since then, however, prices have started to fall. This is because golf ball diving, seen as a good way of making a lot of money, was being carried out by too many people and supply outstripped demand. Also, the economic crash in the latter part of this decade meant that there were fewer rich bankers taking a day off for a round of golf.

Hand Colouring of Photographs

HAND COLOURING OF PHOTOS IS seen by its modern-day practitioners as creating an artistic effect that colour film cannot provide. Also known as hand painting and overpainting, it is a method of manually applying colour to black and white photographs as an art form. The resulting image is usually kept under glass to protect it.

The media used in this process include dyes, watercolours and coloured pencils, which are applied to the surface of the photograph often using brushes, cotton swabs or air brushes. Oils, pastels and crayons have also been used. Hand coloured photographs were at their most popular during the nineteenth century before the introduction of colour photography, when some firms specialised in the practice. Women were generally employed to carry out these tasks. Most professional portrait photographers offered a hand-coloured option, sometimes colouring the photos themselves, although others considered hand colouring to be a blasphemy to their craft. Some artists disapproved of hand colouring, believing it to be "an uncreative way to create works of art", as an article by an academic at the University of Texas puts it. Maverick portrait artists used overpainted photography to pass off as their own artwork.

The early daguerreotype method was also hand coloured soon after its invention in 1839. Only three years after Daguerre revealed his invention to the public, the first patent in the US for the colourisation of daguerreotypes was granted to Benjamin R. Stevens and Lemuel Morse. For every photographic medium that arose, a hand colouring method was devised.

Hand colouring was the easiest and most effective way to produce colour photographs until the introduction of Kodachrome colour film in the mid-twentieth century. Although colour photography became possible in the late nineteenth century it was an expensive and difficult process.

The period between 1900 and 1940 can be seen as the "golden age" of hand colouring of photos. This included landscape photography as well as portraiture. Between 1915 and 1925, the process was very popular in Canada and the USA, amongst other places. They were seen by the public as affordable wedding gifts, birthday gifts or holiday souvenirs. However, with the onset of the Great Depression in 1929, and the resulting drop in the size of the middle class, sales of the photographs tumbled. Despite this, skilled photographers continued to create beautiful hand coloured photographs. One of these was Luiz Marques (1899-1978) whose work is housed in the University of Houston, Texas as well as in Mexico.

Although by the 1950s colour film had all but ended the process of hand colouring photographs, during the 1970s there was somewhat of a revival in it, carried out by such artists as Elizabeth Lennard, Kathy Vargas and Rita Dibert. The combination of photography and painting techniques was also practised by Robert Rauschenberg and others. During the 1970s hand colouring was used in some fashion work and on record sleeves such as David Bowie's Ziggy Stardust album and those of Led Zeppelin, Roxy Music and AC-DC. It was also used on some book covers. There was now a new reason for colourisation, which was to reinterpret images in a way that colour films could not.

Some artists continue to colour photos in the traditional way, using such media as watercolours, oils, crayons and pastels. Colourist Judith Monroe, in an interview with *unblinkingeye.com*, said that she has used all these methods. Photographic dyes are also used, for example by Andrew Sanderson, known as one of the world's best hand colourists. The main concern of a hand colourist is that one's choice of media should take well to the surface being used, and that the artist is comfortable in applying it. Generally, media that have transparency and allow the detail of the photo to show through are preferred.

Dyes originally designed for use in the textile industry were first used to hand colour photographs in the 1860s. These are generally applied by staining the print rather than painting it so that the detail of the photo will be visible. Blotting paper is used to remove excess dye from the surface of the photograph.

According to *Ilford.com*, Sanderson uses a drop of washing up liquid on his palette, of which he applies a tiny amount to each colour he mixes, to ensure an even covering on the photo. He says it is better to apply the colours in daylight rather than artificial light, otherwise the finished product will look wrong when viewed in natural light.

As Sanderson explains, he first came across hand coloured photos in the late seventies and these were by a Yorkshire photographer named Porl Medlock. This inspired him to follow in his footsteps and take up colourisation for himself. He did not want to copy Medlock, so he took up the use of dyes instead of coloured pencils. "My first attempts were rather heavy handed, and I was plagued with patchy colours" said Sanderson. Because of this he chose to dilute the dyes before using them and gradually built up the colours, which helped to even out their application, but they still needed to be applied carefully. Sanderson added: "My first prints were quite small, but I soon progressed to doing everything at 10 x 8 inches (25.4 x 20.3 cm) and found this an ideal size to work with."

At the time he came across Medlock's work, Sanderson, then a student, was becoming disillusioned with colour prints. "The colours were either garish or pale and inaccurate" he says. This encouraged him to take up hand colouring as a way of gaining more accuracy and control of images, with the sharpness that black and white photography provides. He went on to colour even larger pictures that were 20 x 16 inches (50.8 x 40.6 cm). This took a great deal of time, working slowly and carefully, but Sanderson said he finds the work relaxing.

When using dyes, one of the most difficult parts of hand colourisation is to get an even colour over a large area such as the sky. Skin tones are also difficult to reproduce accurately. Sanderson prefers to apply these dyes to a spare print before committing himself to the end result.

Coloured pencils are also a popular choice for the hand colouring of photographs, as used by Medlock, but they should always be used on matte paper. They will also obscure the image if applied too copiously, which means that highly detailed photographs may not be suitable.

Judith Monroe had been using oils, but with two toddlers in the house, she decided this was too much of a hazard, so she started using coloured pencils instead. She chooses to apply the colours to matte, fibre-based paper which she believes produces the best results.

Monroe explained that although any coloured pencils may be used, higher quality artist's pencils will be easier to use because they have softer textures. She uses harder pencils for a final layer, as a way of "burnishing" the photograph. Since pigments in pencils can't be mixed like paints, the process of getting the right colour involves layering the colours in the same way as one would when creating a coloured pencil sketch. "The final result can be an image with amazing depth of colour" says Monroe.

She later moved on to using watercolours and added that although they can be used on almost any photographic surface, of all the media she has used, these "are the most challenging to control". She goes on to advise the would-be colourist: "I would encourage some schooling and practice before working on your photographs."

Today, the effect of hand colouring can be simulated using image manipulation software such as Adobe Photoshop, which means that colourisation is more readily available to the amateur photographer.

Iceberg Movers

AFTER THE *TITANIC* DISASTER IN 1912, a group of North American and European countries joined forces to make sure the same thing never happened again. They established an organisation called the International Ice Patrol. Today it uses satellite data, radar and aeroplanes to monitor the movement of icebergs. The IIP informs the maritime industry about potentially hazardous icebergs and which sea lanes are safe to navigate. It also tracks the bergs that are coming dangerously close to oil and gas rigs. These can be huge chunks of Greenland's glaciers, which move with the currents into the North Atlantic and become a danger to oil rigs off Newfoundland's coast. Unlike ship's captains, rigs cannot manoeuvre out of the way.

When an iceberg drifts too close to a sea platform, an anchor handling tug supply (AHTS) vessel is used by ice management contractors to tow it away. These contractors use tow ropes that are "eight inches [20cm] in diameter and a quarter of a mile [400 metres] long", according to *amusingplanet.com,* which are necessary to move the immense structures that are the icebergs. The vessels used in this task are kept at least half a mile (800 metres) away from the icebergs in case they flip over in transit, which can be disastrous. This can sometimes happen because some have undersea projections which are not visible from the surface. If this happens, the berg can slice through the boat as well as generating large waves which may overcome the vessel. On occasion, a tow rope may break, which is another possible reason for the berg to roll over.

It can take up to 72 hours to tow a berg out of harm's way since it takes about 10 miles (16 km) to accelerate to a speed of one U.S. nautical mile (1.85 km) per hour. Bergs are not towed all the way to safety, just to a position where the currents will carry them past the rig without incident. In cases where an iceberg cannot be towed, water cannon are used to push them away.

Iceberg towing occurs frequently in the Arctic in the vicinity of oil rigs. Some contractors shift 70 to 100 icebergs per year. A unique way of moving icebergs off Newfoundland was to haul one ashore, and to make Iceberg Vodka out of the pristine meltwater. Although towing icebergs is not exactly a high-tech business, oil rig workers off the east coast of Canada are reassured by the knowledge that towing ships are ready to assist them.

Every year around Greenland's glaciers between 20,000 and 40,000 new icebergs are formed. They are moved by the currents and arrive in the North Atlantic the following season. Fewer than 500 of these bergs drift south towards the coast of Newfoundland and become a menace to shipping and oil installations. As they travel, they splinter and fracture and smaller pieces of ice knowns as "growlers" or "bergy bits" break off them. The *Titanic* itself encountered an iceberg south of Boston, Massachusetts in 1912 and as recently as 2002 a shrimp trawler *BCM Atlantic* struck an iceberg off the coast of Labrador and sank in five minutes.

Seafaring vessels are not so much endangered by the large bergs, which can generally be easily seen and avoided, but are more at risk from the growlers or other fractured pieces of the bergs. These are much more difficult to spot in the North Atlantic waves and are not detectable by radar. In some parts of the ocean, there is a multitude of these frozen hazards. Icebergs do not just collide with things, but as *shipsandoil.com* puts it: "If deep enough, they gouge out troughs in the sea-bed. . . varying from 32.8 ft to 492 ft (10 to 150 m) wide. Any pipelines or fibre optic cables in their path would be gathered up like so much spaghetti."

A small deviation of an iceberg is all that is needed to avoid collisions and causing them to deviate has become an industry of iceberg towing using the AHTS vessels. Jeff Mullin, featured in *shipsandoil.com*, is the captain of one of these boats and has 3,937 ft (1,200 metres) of wire at his disposal, along with 14,000 horse- power engines. On one occasion he tackled a berg

1000 ft (307 metres) long and 770 ft (235 m) wide that rose 32 ft 10 inches (10 metres) above the surface of the ocean. As they towed it, they had 7,381,548 tons (7,500,000 tonnes) on the wire. Occasionally a wire will become detached from the berg and there is also the risk of the iceberg turning over. Smaller, fractured pieces of ice are moved by "prop washing", where by repeatedly backing close, the ship's propeller is used to create a strong wave able to move the berg a distance of half a mile (800m) or more.

Although it has proved practical to move icebergs for short distances, French engineer Georges Mougin has another idea which he has been working on since the 1970s. While 1.1 billion people in the world are without access to clean drinking water, billions of gallons or litres of freshwater melts away from icebergs that have broken off the glaciers of Greenland into the salt-water of the sea. In 1977, Mougin joined forces with other engineers and a polar explorer on a plan to relocate an iceberg to Saudi Arabia in a venture called "Iceberg Transport International".

Working for the Saudi government, they planned to "wrap a million-tonne [984,548 ton] iceberg in sailcloth and plastic and tow it from the Arctic to the Red Sea", (*fastcompany.com*, a Business and Innovation website), for an estimated cost of $100 million. In a demonstration of his abilities Mougin transported a "mini berg", weighing 4,409 lb (two tonnes), by helicopter, plane and truck from Alaska to Iowa. When the berg arrived, ice was chipped off the block to chill drinks for delegates at a conference he was holding there. However, the conference broke up in acrimony over cost and feasibility and the plan did not come to fruition.

It is reported that 35 years later Mougin had teamed up with the Abu Dhabi based National Advisor Bureau, an environmental consultancy, to re-launch his idea, this time moving an iceberg from the Antarctic to the United Arab Emirates. Abdulla Al-Shehi,, director of the Bureau, has reportedly said that tapping the freshwater reserves of an iceberg is an environmentally friendly way of solving the UAE's water shortage. The gulf state is covered by desert and is one of the world's most arid countries. The UAE relies on diminishing groundwater resources and the desalination of sea water, an expensive and inefficient process that pollutes the sea by returning unwanted brine to it. "We plan to tow icebergs located north of

Antarctica some 9,200 km [5,716 miles] to the shores of Fujairah", Al-Shehi is quoted as saying in the *Dominion Post.*

Mougin and his associates plan to move one iceberg initially and then, if successful, to go back for more. The icebergs they have chosen are, on average, nearly 1mile 1521 yds (three km) long and 984 ft (300 metres) deep. They aim to tow the bergs to the Gulf of Oman at Fujairah, which is the most easterly of the seven Emirates that comprise the UAE. Here the water is deep enough to accommodate the berg. The bergs they are interested in are the optimum size ones – not too big, not too small – and craggy, irregular icebergs are best avoided. Tabular shaped bergs are preferred, because they are easiest to tow and are least likely to fracture. The ice would be wrapped in an insulated covering and attached to a barge which would follow sea currents to give it extra momentum. Mougin worked with French design company Dassault Systemes who provided 3D computer simulations and expects to lose 30 per cent of the iceberg through the year-long journey.

Once the bergs had arrived at Fujairah, they would be anchored 15 miles (25km) off the shoreline, where the ice would be gradually chipped away using a custom-built ice crusher. The ice removed from the bergs would then be transported ashore using floating tanks, ready to be used as drinking water. According to the *Dominion Post*, Al-Shehi has said "the icebergs could hold enough drinking water for one million people for five years."

Mougin at this point believed he could now achieve what he had failed to do in 1977. When Dassault Systemes first ran the simulation, the results were disappointing. Their simulated berg got caught up in big currents for weeks while it melted away. When they tried again, this time in a different part of the season, "it just worked", Dassault Systemes' Cedric Simard told *fastcompany.com*. "They say it's like a nutshell towing a mountain -- and yet it's possible", he added.

Spurred on by the success of the simulation, Mougin ploughed ahead with his plans including pilot schemes to tow mini bergs a short distance and creating a new company. However, so far, he has not been able to say how much the operation to move an iceberg would cost and at the time of writing the project is still work in progress.

Illusionists

THE FIRST KNOWN ACCOUNT OF a magic trick dates from the sixteenth century BC. An Egyptian document, now in a museum in Berlin, describes the magician Dedi, who according to the BBC series *QI Quite Interesting*, "pulls the heads off a goose, and duck and an ox, and then restores them to life, though he refuses to do the trick on a human prisoner". Modern day magician David Copperfield has performed this trick with a duck and a goose too.

One of the earliest magic tricks to be documented was the "cup and balls" trick. It dates back at least 2,000 years. The trick is typically done with three cups and three balls, which inexplicably move from cup to cup. This trick is used to measure the abilities of conjurers and was performed by Prince Charles in his induction to the Inner Magic Circle.

In the early days of illusionism, there were no conjuring handbooks and "magicians" would pass on their secrets to the next generation of their trade. The first French conjuring book was published in 1584 by Jean Prevost, called *La Premiere Partie des Subtiles et Plaisantes Inventions* (The First Part of Subtle and Pleasant Tricks), suggesting a second volume was on the way, but no record of it exists. Popular card tricks are not included.

The first book of tricks in English is "The Discoverie of Witchcraft" by Reginald Scot, published later in 1584. It was designed to show that magic was not really done by witchcraft, and magicians in fact conducted elaborate tricks. As well as refuting the church's allegations against people it saw as witches, Scot explained that tricks such as the cup and ball trick and those with coins, cards, handkerchiefs and paper were not really magic but performed with sleight of hand. Nevertheless, King James I did not like the publication, and had all known copies burnt. Churchmen were hostile to and against all forms of conjuring, including theatrical amusements.

According to *The Illustrated History of Magic* by Milbourne and Maurice Christopher: "A girl who ripped a handkerchief apart and restored it, before a large audience, was tried for witchcraft in Cologne in the fifteenth century." Also, the book relates that, after conjuring performances in Padua and Mantua in Italy, a man named Reatis was arrested and tortured until he explained his sleight of hand and the assistance of his associates.

Although the practice of illusionism dates back many centuries, its heyday was in the nineteenth century theatre and fairgrounds. The Victorian era provided the optimum conditions for illusionism as technology developed alongside an insatiable curiosity for the inexplicable and the strange. The days before movies and the cinema can be seen as the "Golden Age of Theatre". Here the most popular shows were performed by magicians. Most of the tricks carried out today date from this time.

One of the venues for such theatrical performances was the Egyptian Hall in London. Performances were also held at the Royal Polytechnic. These two venues became dedicated to magic shows and well-known magicians such as George Alfred Cooke and John Neville Maskelyne performed there. The Polytechnic was best known for its astonishing magic lantern shows, especially after 1848 when it was under the management of John Henry Pepper. The Egyptian Hall was a popular venue for a wide range of illusionist performances throughout the nineteenth century until its closure in 1905. The theatre setting allowed the conjuring to become increasingly elaborate and complex because it was suited to using machinery and hidden assistants.

To add to the mysticism of their acts, some conjurers went by Eastern names (such as Ching Ling Foo and Chung Ling Soo). The best performances were so convincing that audiences believed they were seeing true magic, and not illusionism. Audiences of the day were led to believe that much of the magic they saw had its origins in the mysterious East.

By the 1870s, Maskelyne and Cooke were at the forefront of illusionism and other sorts of entertainment such as ventriloquism. They also promoted the acts of up and coming magicians, but remarkably refused the American magician Harry Houdini the opportunity to perform at the Egyptian Hall in 1898, just two years before he made his name at another London venue. Houdini is the best remembered magician of his day. However, another prominent illusionist of the nineteenth century was The Great Lafayette, who fell into obscurity because he did not live long enough to transfer his skills to the "silver screen".

During the second half of the twentieth century, magic was easily transferred from the silver screen to the television screen, which brought about new opportunities for deception and provided illusionism with much larger audiences. However, most television magicians perform to a live audience at the same time, which reassures the television viewer that the illusions are not done using post-production visual effects.

Despite the fact that many of the principles of stage magic date back to at least the nineteenth century, modern magicians have vanished buildings as large as the Taj Mahal and even the Statue of Liberty. In November 2000 the building sometimes described as "the most beautiful in the world", the Taj Mahal in India, was made to vanish before astounded onlookers by magician P.C. Sorcar Jr. Sorcar was assisted by his daughter and they made the building disappear for two minutes.

The trick was performed about 1312 ft (400 m) from the Taj, on the banks of the River Yamuna. "I just kept the Taj away from your eyes. It was a perfect illusion", Sorcar is quoted as saying by the BBC. Sorcar has also been credited with making a moving train disappear, as well as vanishing Kolkata's Victoria Memorial and making an aircraft disappear in Japan. He explained that illusionism has been in his family for eight generations. There was "nothing supernatural" about this vanishing act, he said. "This is all science, the science of controlling the mind and the willpower to create a psychic balance with the environment."

One of modern magician David Copperfield's most well-known tricks was to make the Statue of Liberty disappear to a live television audience in 1983. To accomplish the trick, he raised a huge sheet of fabric to hide the statue, and then lowered it to show that the statue had disappeared. A helicopter manned with a camera crew even passed through the space to show that it really was empty. Once this was achieved, he made the statue reappear. It is said that Copperfield meant to emphasise "how precious liberty is and how easily it can be lost".

As well as the British Indian magician P.J. Sorcar Jr, born in 1946, modern day magicians include the British magician Paul Daniels (1938-2016). Well known for his long running television show, he was the first non-American to receive the award of Magician of the Year in 1983 from the Hollywood Academy of Magical Arts.

The American magician Criss Angel, born in 1967, is also world famous. He won the International Magicians Society Magician of the Year award a record breaking five times. They also named him Magician of the Decade and even Magician of the Century. His popular television show Criss Angel Mindfreak, which featured a variety of tricks and conjuring feats, ran for five years. As *totallyhistory.com* puts it: "His signature tricks are making doves appear to materialise and fly from his hands, levitation and disappearing acts."

David Blaine, also an American, has performed several acts during his career which put his life at risk. One of these was called Frozen in Time, in which he was sealed up in a large block of ice for a little less than 64 hours, which left him unable to walk for a month. On another occasion he stood for 35 hours atop a 100 ft (30.5 m) tall, 22-inch (56cm) wide pillar. He named this trick Vertigo.

American Dorothy Dietrich is a stage magician and escapologist described by *abracadabra.com* as being "the first woman to catch a bullet in her mouth, and the first woman to escape from a straitjacket whilst suspended in the air by a burning rope". She was dubbed as one of the eight most notable magicians of the twentieth century by *Columbia Encyclopedia* and is called "the female Houdini" because of her success in escapology acts similar to his. She also performed one trick that Houdini was not willing to perform, the Jinxed Bullet Escape Stunt. Dietrich was inspired to become an escapologist by reading a biography of Houdini as a child. She has made many television appearances and participates in a travelling Houdini show.

To become a successful magician, one must be highly skilled and well trained, and it is an art that is shrouded in secrecy. The best known and most intriguing tricks are a closely guarded secret, known only to a few. As time goes on there are always more talented and up and coming magicians to step into the shoes of those who have gone before them.

Japanning

JAPANNING ORIGINATED IN THE SEVENTEENTH century as a European imitation of Asian lacquer work, the finest of which came from Japan. The original oriental version of the process used naturally occurring lacquers that were highly polished. The lacquers were elaborately decorated in gold. By the late 1600s, European demand for it was too great to be catered for solely by the export trade, and production started in Italy. It was first applied to furniture and later to smaller metal items for decoration and protection purposes. In earlier times a similar process was known as India ware but it was japanning that really caught on.

It is most often associated with a heavy black lacquer that has a similar effect to that of enamel paint. In fact, japanning is often seen as synonymous with black colouration, although green, red and blue items can also be found. In its traditional form the surface is overpainted with gold designs and pictures.

The Italian technique of japanning was particularly sought after. The manufacture of japanned items also took place in Britain, France and the Low Countries. Colonial Boston was also a centre of excellence in production of japanned goods in America.

The art of japanning by Europeans developed over the next two centuries, as new varnishing methods and materials became available. Japanned objects are made with a variety of materials and varnishes were applied in multiple layers. Oil varnishes were developed in the early eighteenth century. These were applied first to wood and later to new materials such as tin plate, and later papier maché which was invented in 1773.

This meant that japanning could now be applied to objects such as carriages and also a variety of household items, and in particular, tea trays. In fact, Japanning can be applied to almost any surface, including wooden furniture from large pieces to small objects such as boxes.

In the 1720s the first place where the construction of tin plate took place in the UK was Pontypool in Wales, and the town became the leading centre for the production of japanned ware in Britain. The trade was very well established in the West Midlands by the late eighteenth century and was centred around Bilston and Wolverhampton although it did not fully develop in Wolverhampton until the mid-nineteenth century. The difference between the two towns regarding japanning was that papier maché work was not carried out in Bilston. The japanned ware produced there went mainly to the cheaper export market, especially Spain and South America, and the work there was designed with these markets in mind.

Some companies produced "blanks" which were to be japanned later by another business, while others specialised in the japanning itself. The largest companies always did both. The objects destined for japanning would, in the case of tin plate, be made of shaped pieces of iron covered with tin which were then soldered and riveted together to make the desired construction. For a long time, this was done by hand, but in the 1840s steam powered machinery was introduced to carry out the task, although some small businesses used simpler stamping machines.

Papier maché was not really mashed up paper at all. It was made firstly in a "pasting shop" by placing a sheet of paper over a mould in the shape of the objects that were to be made, or by laying them flat for panels. Further layers of paper were applied, up to 120 times in some cases. Each layer was thoroughly pasted with a mixture of glue and flour. The items were then placed in a stove to dry them out, which had to be done several times where the items were at their thickest. Some items, such as hollow ones, were constructed in parts which were glued together and to which further layers of paper would then be applied. Once the object was made, it was soaked in oil and dried once again for about a day and a half. According to

Wolverhampton City Council, the material that was created in this way "was not dissimilar to wood or a modern hardboard and could be sawn, planed, filed and generally worked much like wood".

The resulting objects whether made of tin plate or papier maché were next sent to a "blacking shop" or "varnishing shop" where several coats of varnish were applied. Each time a layer of varnish was added the object had again to be stove dried. This took longer at lower temperatures in the case of wood or papier maché. Tin plate was dried hotter for a shorter time.

Once the object had a suitable glow to its surface, it was sent to the gilding shop where highly skilled craftsmen would apply gold decoration to it. (Women were not generally permitted to participate in this stage of the work and were usually restricted to the pasting shop.) Next, some items were sent on to the painting shop where painters would usually copy from the work of a master craftsman, who could just as easily work with pottery as with japanned ware. Some of these men were highly paid. Finally, the objects were sent to the varnishing shop for a last coating with a clear varnish to protect the artwork and then, after much polishing, would acquire the desired glossy finish of japanned ware.

Experts in japanning were well paid and some took up lucrative offers to work abroad, for example in the USA where they were employed to help set up japanning businesses. However, the work was hazardous to health, because of the effect of smoke and fumes on workers and the risk of fire was quite high.

Once the manufacture of the products had been completed, larger firms employed travelling salesmen, who would often be senior partners in the business. Smaller manufacturers had to sell the goods themselves.

Many men, women and children made their living in the trade. By 1818 trade directories list 20 japanning businesses in Wolverhampton and 15 in Bilston. According to Samuel Timmins' *Birmingham and the Midlands Hardware District* (1886) there were 2,000 people employed in the japanning and tinplate industries in Wolverhampton and Bilston at the time.

The size of these businesses varied from a plethora of family workshops to a small number of large factories, which employed over 250 people in some cases. While some of the smaller businesses specialised in construction or decoration, most of the larger companies did everything under one roof.

Japanning was at the height of its popularity in the mid-nineteenth century, and was seen in most middle-class homes, but by the 1880s, tastes had begun to change, and the japanning and tinplate industry went into decline. It was replaced in many cases by electroplating, which was a new and burgeoning industry.

In order to adapt, some japanners switched to "enamelling, electroplating, and the manufacture of copper and brass coal scuttles, fire screens and kettles", according to *wolverhamptonhistory.org*. Others changed their focus from decorative to utilitarian items. Here the japanning was applied mainly to protect the metal and decoration was minimal. These objects included items from cash boxes to bicycles as well as the new market for motor vehicles.

Some even manufactured bicycles themselves. The most prosperous of these was John Marston, whose factory began manufacturing bicycles in 1887. As *wolverhamptonhistory.org* describes: "This part of the business quickly became more profitable than the manufacturing of decorative japanned ware which was soon abandoned, and the factory was renamed Sunbeam Cycle Works." By the 1920s, the market for decorative japanned ware had dried up and the industry was almost obsolete.

Japanning as it occurs today is a term almost exclusively applied to the decoration of grandfather clocks with acrylic paints. The practice of decorating the clock faces in this way first gained widespread popularity in the late eighteenth century. Early examples are recognisable for the simplicity of the designs and the use of floral motifs. In the early nineteenth century the fashion was for depicting "shells, geometric patterns, local scenes and historical events", according to the clock manufacturers *Comitti*. These added significantly to the decorative appeal of grandfather clocks. Some clock manufactures such as *Comitti* continue to employ skilled craftspeople to carry out this work today, using traditional methods.

Knocker-up

THE KNOCKER-UP, ALSO KNOWN AS the knocker-upper, has been described as "one of the most hated men in nineteenth century England", according to *Beachcombing's Bizarre History Blog*. The job was widespread in Britain and Ireland from the early days of the industrial revolution until the beginning of the twentieth century. Before alarm clocks were affordable for factory workers, this was a popular way for people to be roused early enough to get to work on time. Those arriving late for work, even by a few minutes, would have their pay docked, which meant that getting to work on time could be a matter of life or death.

The role of the knocker-up found its way into contemporary literature such as Charles Dickens's *Great Expectations*, where a brief description of this type of work can be found in the introduction.

Knocker-uppers would rise before their customers in order to tap their bedroom windows with a stick that had a knob or a wire attached to it, to wake them in the morning. In many cases their customers' working day would start at six am. Often the sticks were made of light bamboo and had to be long enough to reach the upper windows. At least one who took on this work, East Ender Mary Smith, was known to use a pea shooter. Some people would use a "snuffer-outer" which was an instrument designed for snuffing out gas lamps at dawn.

The knocker-up would be paid a few pence a week to provide this service. Usually the knocker-up would not desist until sure that the customer had awoken properly and their face had appeared at the window. The job was often done by people who had retired from their regular jobs or by police constables looking to supplement their income while out on their morning patrols. The job also ran in families such as mother and daughter.

Customers would, in some cases, put out a slate with the time they were due to be woken written on it, or mark the pavement in chalk, for the benefit of the knocker-up. All it took was a shower of rain to wash these markings away, so some knockers-up put billboards outside houses which advertised their services and stated the wake-up time of the customer.

In the northern mill towns, where people worked shifts, or in London's docklands where workers' hours varied according to the tides, knockers-up were familiar sight at different times of the day. Some factory owners employed the knocker-up themselves to make sure their workers arrived on time.

Quite a lot of people were employed in this sort of work in the major industrial areas of Britain such as London and Manchester. But this occurred in smaller towns too, such as Poole in Dorset where a knocker-up affectionately known as Granny Cousins could be found waking the brewery workers in the later part of the nineteenth century and through to her retirement in 1918.

A problem for the knocker-up was to make sure that people in houses adjoining those of their customers did not get woken up for free. Sometimes these people were grateful for the free service, sometimes not. The solution was to use a stick with which to tap the windows of their customers, loudly enough to wake them but not their neighbours. One of the hazards of the knocker-up's job was grumpy members of the public who were angry, sleepy and sometimes hung-over. These people would on occasion drench knocker-ups with a bucket of water, even if they had employed their services. It may have been a curious custom but knocking-up provided an honest living for anyone willing to rise earlier than their fellows and work in the outdoors whatever the weather.

According to *digging-history.com*: "At the Bishop of London's residence, Fulham Palace, the lodge keeper began knocking up the domestic help at around 5.30 am". He used a 15ft (4.6 m) pole known as a "rousing stave" and would persist until he got a more or less grateful response from the servants. A similar stave was used during church services by the "sluggard-waker" to keep the congregation awake.

In the USA knocking up was seen as a quaint British practice. Here it was unusual for workers' houses to be more than two storeys high and the street design, with the accommodation more closely packed together, meant that a knocker-up would quickly be able to rouse the inhabitants of a whole street. This meant that in the US knocking up was not a profitable exercise.

An American even came up with a tongue twister about the person who knocked-up the knocker-up, which went as follows: "One morning a lad went into the factory at quarter past seven and the manager saw him and said: 'Well. Johnny, why are you so late?' The boy began to cry and said: 'Well, Sir, it's a case of this. Our knocker-up has a knocker-up to knock him up at four am and our knocker-up's knocker-up didn't knock our knocker-up up, so your knocker-up didn't come to knock us up.'" In most cases, however the knocker-up could be relied on to carry out a regular and timely service.

In some cases, knocker-ups saved the lives of their customers. An example of this was reported in the *London Evening Standard* where, having discovered that a house was on fire, a knocker-up sounded the alarm, and "two women saved themselves by sliding down sheets into the street". "The building was gutted, but the occupants were saved thanks to their neighbouring knocker-up" as described by *digging-history.com*.

The work of the knocker-up was generally regular and provided a steady income, but when strikes took place at the factories, the knocker-up was without work. One man was had up in court for theft and pleaded that "because of the cotton lock-out nobody wanted my services and I was starving." Another man who was adversely affected by the cotton lock-out had been working as a knocker-up for 40 years. Suddenly he found himself without any customers. Knocking up was his only occupation; he had no other means of support. Unlike the factory workers, knockers-up had no trade unions to support them and the strikes left them out of pocket. In some places, though, they banded together to demand advance payment.

An exceptional type of person was needed to make a living rising in the early hours to wake up others for their day's work. On such man was Henry Wood, who, when he became unwell, was nursed back to health by Florence

Nightingale. He seemed well suited to the challenges of his work. Rising every morning at four am he would go out into the streets and tap the windows of cotton workers who had paid him a few pence a week for the service. He would do this however bad the weather but remained "hale and hearty", according to those who knew him.

Many knockers-up were dismayed when an Act of Parliament in 1913 declared them to be uninsurable along with "men who put burrs under the wheels of vehicles, cover the horses, adjust their nose-bags, while their drivers are in a shop".

When the First World War broke out the demand for the services of the knocker-up increased substantially in places such as Lancashire where military-related industries were located. In Britain the practice persisted well into the twentieth century, by which time the rest of the world had long since moved on to using alarm clocks.

During the Second World War knockers-ups were still employed in some areas of England. By early 1951 there were still a few knockers-up employed to rouse the railway workers in the town of Derby. However, on 4 August 1951, the practice there was finally abolished.

Ever since the start of the railway age, knockers-ups have trudged through snow, fog and rain to wake the workers in the big railway towns. But the railway managements saw the opportunity to save a great deal of money by asking the workers to rouse themselves. The knockers-up were convinced the resulting chaos would mean they got their jobs back within a month. This proved not to be the case and the decision signified the near demise of the long tradition of the knocker-up, although in a few places, it persisted until the early 1970s.

Limning

ORIGINALLY, LIMNING WAS THE HAND illustration of manuscripts, often carried out by monks, until the invention of printing, when this practice died out. The word limner is derived from the medieval word *luminer*, meaning an illustrator of manuscripts.

However, from the beginning of the sixteenth century the term usually applied to miniature portrait painters. This continued until the nineteenth century when the term became almost obsolete. The earliest portrait miniaturists were well known book illustrators such as the Frenchman Jean Fouquet (1420-1481), widely seen as the inventor of the portrait miniature, and Flemish artist Simon Bening (1483-1561).

From the 1460s, hand-written books had to compete with printed books. Limners such as Simon Bening nevertheless continued to practise the art of manuscript illustration for those who could afford these luxury items, but also offered portrait miniatures to their customers. Some of these were for private worship, while others were seen as desirable objects which could be used as love tokens or symbols of political affiliation.

Portrait miniatures began to emerge at the French and English Courts in the first half of the sixteenth century. They were generally painted onto vellum (calf skin) until the eighteenth century when painting watercolours on ivory or using enamel became popular.

Despite their size, they had a realistic looking effect. The earliest of these examples were painted by two Dutchmen, Jean Clouet (1483-1520), who worked in France and Lucas Horenbout (1490-1544), who worked in

England as Royal Painter to Henry VIII from 1531. It is a widely held view that Horenbout brought the art of the portrait miniature to England for the first time. His father Gerald and his sister Susannah were also miniature portrait artists. Twenty-three miniatures are attributed to him of which seven are of the king, thought to have been created for members of the royal family and the king's mistresses. One picture is believed to have been intended for King Francis I of France, sometime friend and rival of the English monarch.

Miniatures were useful to the monarchy who could bestow them on people as a sign of royal favour. In many cases the recipient would have to provide the frame and locket at their own expense. The casings were usually made of ivory or gold. The other main use for portrait miniatures was as love tokens. Customers paid between £3 and £5 for these in Elizabethan times, equivalent to £900-£1,300 in today's terms.

In the 1580s the wealthier subjects of Elizabeth I started to carry portrait miniatures of their monarch "as a sign of loyalty, at a time when Protestant England was threatened by Catholic Spain", according to the Victoria and Albert Museum. It became fashionable for subjects of Elizabeth I to wear her portrait miniatures almost as a talisman. Sometimes people would keep these in highly decorated containers rather than actually wear them.

Nicholas Hilliard (1547-1619) painted a renowned miniature of Queen Elizabeth when she was aged 39 in 1572 which is now in the collection of the National Portrait Gallery. The Queen is shown as youthful looking and is dressed in her royal livery with a jewelled head-dress and a closely fitting ruff.

In his treatise *The Art of Limning*, Hilliard explains his methods and processes, as well as how to make such necessities such as the pigments and gum that he uses to create portrait miniatures. He emphasises his belief that limning is a gentleman's art and is not suitable for people of lower social standing.

Hilliard spent two years in France from 1576 to 1578 which meant that his subsequent work was influenced by the French style. In the 1590s he produced some full-length miniatures of which perhaps the best known is titled Unknown Young Man Leaning Against a Tree Among Roses. "This eight-inch (20 cm) portrait depicts a young man, possibly Robert Devereux, Earl of Essex. The youth is interwoven with leafy branches and roses, 'the Tudor symbol'", according to *decodedpast.com.* This portrait was an example of Hilliard's work at the peak of his career and is recognised as one of the finest works of art of the Elizabethan era.

Hilliard was the first Englishman of international repute to serve the royal court as an official Warrant Holder. Before his time most court artists came from abroad, such as Rembrandt and Hans Holbein. The royal appointment was not a paid job and Hilliard had to run a workshop in the City of London to make his living. Here his pupils included Roland Lockley and Isaac Oliver, but many historians believe that his miniature portraiture has never been surpassed. As well as the Queen, his customers included Sir Walter Raleigh and Sir Francis Drake. He is described by historian Ema Auerbach in her work *Nicholas Hilliard* as "the most eminent miniaturist of the age".

Elizabeth gave the miniature known as the Drake Jewel as a gift to Sir Francis Drake. This was probably in recognition of the part he played in defeating the Spanish Armada in 1588. The jewel consisted of two portraits of Elizabeth I and her emblem, the phoenix.

As Elizabeth got older, Hilliard was faced with the dilemma of how best to represent her without showing that she had aged. In order to deal with this problem, he portrayed very little facial detail and distracted the onlooker away from her face by accentuating her resplendent costumes and ornate jewellery as well as her extravagant hair styles. In order to avoid showing her black teeth, Hilliard painted the queen with her mouth closed. To disguise her ageing facial features, the Queen also wore heavy makeup. Hilliard's portraits of her at this time came to be known as the "mask of youth portraits".

Many examples of Hilliard's work remain in good condition today together with the cases that he designed himself, and from these portraits we have evidence of the fashions of the royal court and the elite class.

As a publication by the V&A states: "James I, who ascended the throne in 1603, learned from Elizabeth the propaganda power of miniatures and during his reign Nicholas Hilliard and Isaac Oliver produced many miniatures of the King and his family."

Later in the seventeenth century, another prominent English painter of miniature portraits was Samuel Cooper (1609-1672) who set up in business in 1642 and painted by appointment to Charles I until the king's execution in 1649. After this event he continued to work successfully in London, with Oliver Cromwell as one of his clients. After the Restoration in 1660 his role as the leading limner of his day was recognised when in 1663, he was appointed limner to Charles II.

By the mid-1700s, limning was established as a genteel pastime, and its practitioners often had no artistic training. Many were self-taught and some had other jobs. During the late 1760s, a number of young men became prominent limners in England. These included Richard Cosway, the pre-eminent miniaturist of his day. From the age of 14, he was a pupil of William Shipley at his drawing school in London, which was the first of its kind in the city.

During the later eighteenth century, as wealth became more widely distributed due to the creation of the new middle class, resulting from the Industrial Revolution, the market for miniature portraiture grew greatly. Many artists took up limning as a result, providing clients with mementos of those dear to them. Many came to London where a more lucrative market could be found, but some found a buoyant market in their home towns, such as Thomas Hazlehurst of Liverpool.

The last great miniature painter was Queen Victoria's miniaturist, William Charles Ross (1794-1860). His fashionably large portraits were painted to look as if they were done in oils. This effect was produced by meticulous work which few people had the money for. Work produced by other leading miniaturists of the day was just as unaffordable.

The introduction of photography in 1839 meant that accurate likenesses were affordable to the general public and according to Peter Cox, a curator at the National Portrait Gallery, coincidentally fashions were less colourful at the time. Many miniaturists adapted to use photography instead of painting, but younger artists rarely pursued careers as miniaturists, and so the art form fell out of fashion. However, Cox tells me practitioners still operate today and there is a society promoting the art, namely the Royal Miniature Society (*www.royal-miniature-society.org.uk*)

Lion Taming

THE FIRST CIRCUS OF THE "modern" world opened its doors in 1768 on London's South Bank. This consisted of acts by jugglers, clowns, acrobats and equestrian stunt riders, but no big cat taming.

Frenchman Henri Martin shocked audiences in 1819 with the first big cat taming display. He started with a tiger and later went on to work with lions as well. He slowly gained the trust of his animals, venturing into their enclosure little by little.

However, American born circus performer Isaac Van Amburgh popularised the act in the UK and Europe, where he gained "a notorious reputation for his performances with big cats", *(A Brief History of Lion Taming*), touring the continent between 1838-1845. Unlike Martin, he did not try to gain the trust of his animals but instead beat them into submission with a crowbar. Fears for animal safety and welfare existed in the nineteenth century and in 1881 the RSPCA reported that lion taming performances were "an exhibition of cruelty" in which big animals were 'punished into sulky obedience or are made to howl with anger".

After a particularly shocking case of animal cruelty in 1874, when showman Frederick Hewitt forced a pack of hyenas to jump though a ring of fire, there were several successful prosecutions involving the wellbeing of circus animals.

Despite his failings, Van Amburgh is widely credited for "being the first person to put his head into a lion's mouth" (*A Brief History of Lion Taming).* The spectacle quickly caught on as news spread of Van Amburgh's dangerous exploits. Queen Victoria was one of his biggest fans and she even commissioned a portrait of him from artist Edwin Landseer.

The next lion tamer to achieve fame and fortune was Clive Beatty who used not only a whip but a pistol as well, to keep his animals in check. He was a well-known proponent of the 'chair' method of subduing a lion. His performances were at their most notorious in the 1920s, when lion taming was at the peak of its popularity.

It may seem surprising that a lion could be afraid of a chair, which the animal could easily tear to pieces, but in fact the lion is not frightened but confused. Because the lion is so single minded, the chair moving around distracts and makes it lose its train of thought. This means it is unlikely to savage the performer.

It was not only the animals that were exploited by the showmen. Women, non-Europeans, children and disabled people were enlisted to act as lion tamers. Women lion tamers came to be known as 'lion queens'. Not everyone was happy with this and the practice tailed off in the 1850s after Ellen Bright was killed by a tiger whist performing in a circus act. One commentator described this as being a result of her "ill-advised tampering with caged monsters". There was again outrage in 1872 when a disabled lion tamer, Thomas McCarty, was killed by a lion at a circus in Bolton. Despite the dangers that these acts entailed, lion taming could prove to be a successful career for a socially disadvantaged circus performer.

Although there was always some opposition on the grounds of animal welfare, circuses remained popular until the 1950s Today, people who work with lions prefer to call themselves lion trainers. As the twentieth century progressed, audiences came to prefer a less confrontational approach to wild animal training. Performers such as the American entertainers Siegfried and Roy spent many hours trying to understand their animals' personalities and psychology.

Gunther Gebel-Williams (1934-2001) was a hugely popular performer in the USA and is credited with doing away with the man versus beast approach. During the twentieth century, "taming" by force was replaced by the use of trust, repetition, and reward. Although whips are still used, this is only to establish the performer's personal space.

Most circus lions and tigers are born in captivity A typical lion tamer would have worked with his lions since they were cubs. Once the trainer gains the trust of the animal, it can be taught to perform tricks in return for a reward. These techniques are similar to those used by dog owners, but a wild animal such as a lion can never be truly tamed.

Jack Hanna, a keeper at a zoo in Ohio, has underlined this message. People who associate affectionately with lions can never be quite sure about their own safety. As Gunther Gebel-Williams puts it: "A wild animal is like a loaded gun -- it can go off at any time."

Perhaps this is why the circus-going public found lion taming performances so captivating. If it was not for the danger, there would be no thrill in the event.

Despite the fact that fears for animal welfare always existed, it has taken more than 200 years for public attitudes to harden against wild animal training in circuses. The vast majority now believe it is not only cruel but too dangerous as well.

This is bad news for Thomas Chipperfield of Chipperfield's circus, who has come to be known as Britain's last lion tamer. Chipperfield says he prefers the term 'big cat trainer'. He told the *Guardian* that the animals are well treated and 'the circus has evolved with every other animal related industry.'

Chipperfield comes from a long line of lion tamers and he has followed his father into the business. Despite his lack of formal education, Chipperfield is well informed about animal psychology and zoology, knowledgeably quoting many experts in these fields.

He told the *Guardian* that he follows B.F. Skinner's theory of "operant conditioning" which basically means training using repetition and reward. He says he has never hit a lion and that "If I was in a position with a lion where I had to become physical, I've obviously made mistakes somewhere."

He adds that he does not punish them at all as this this would cause them to feel resentful and would be counterproductive. Chipperfield says that training is a slow and careful process which takes many years and is carried out at the lion's own pace.

Animal rights activists are unconvinced. In 2016, an organisation called

Animal Defender International took pictures of Chipperfield's animal enclosures which led to a tabloid scoop concerning cruelty to animals. However, there was no suggestion that Chipperfield had broken the law.

He told the *Guardian* there were frequent checks on his animals' welfare under the terms of the Dangerous Wild Animals Act, as well as his circus licence which requires extra inspections. This is proof, he says, that the animal rights activists have got it wrong.

He adds that although it is true his enclosures are smaller than those provided for zoo animals, his animals have more stimulating lives than those in zoos, which spend most of their time "lounging about". He says that circuses give a greater understanding of animals' abilities and intelligence than zoos do.

Yet his lion taming days may be over. In 2018 the Department for the Environment, Food and Rural Affairs (DEFRA) refused him a licence to perform with his two lions Assegai and Tsavo and this was followed by a legal ban in England in 2020. The spectacle was banned in Scotland in 2018 and the Welsh government followed in 2020. There is also a ban in force in Ireland, and any more lion taming acts in the UK are thought to be unlikely.

Master Sommeliers

ALTHOUGH SOME GREAT SOMMELIERS ARE self-taught, passing the Master Sommelier Diploma is the best route to success in the sale and service of wine. Every year, about two hundred sommeliers from around the world put themselves in for this most demanding test of wine expertise. This takes years of intensive preparation. Improved pay and prestige may follow, but better candidates are looking for personal development rather than future rewards.

The first test they must pass is on wine theory, for which they need a comprehensive knowledge of wine growing regions and styles. Then they move on to the practical service part of the exam, in which they are judged for their courtesy, charm and salesmanship as they wait on a panel of judges who try to catch them out with fussy demands and detailed discussions about wine and vintages. Meanwhile a fake Maître d' checks the time and calls out instructions for them to hurry since other guests are waiting. This part of the exam is designed to see how candidates cope under pressure and lasts for 45 minutes.

As an MS working in a restaurant one should be able to speak knowledgeably about a wine from anywhere in the world, to concisely categorise its ingredients, make a sales pitch, pair it with food and serve it gracefully. However, there is always more to learn and a better name for the Master Sommelier might be the "perpetual student".

Gerard Basset, awarded an OBE for his services to the hospitality industry in 2011, is one of only three people to have achieved both the

Master Sommelier Diploma (in 1989) and the Master of Wine Qualification (1998). He told *Decanter.com*: "In my restaurant experience I've experienced just about everything, from the occasional red wine spill to heart attacks at the table, angry break-ups, epileptic seizures and an impromptu rendition of White Christmas by Bono of Irish band U2."

Bianca Bosker, author of *Cork Dork: A Wine-fuelled Journey into the Art of Sommeliers and the Science of Taste* says she discovered that one candidate took dancing lessons in preparation for the service part of the exam. Another underwent speech therapy to perfect his voice to a "silky baritone", as well as engaging a memory expert to help him remember vineyard names. Others consulted psychologists for advice on how to stay calm under pressure.

Finally, the scariest test of all, is the "blind tasting". In this exam, as Bosker describes it, candidates "must identify three red and three white wines, based on flavour and appearance alone". This includes the species of grape, the vineyard, how long it could be aged, what to eat with it and why, just by the taste and appearance. This must be done within 25 minutes.

Blind tasting is a skill that requires a great deal of practice and memory, more so than ability. This allows one to make a meaningful and objective assessment of a wine's character, free from the hindrance of knowing the label and the price. Candidates must try to describe the wine, estimate its levels of tannin, alcohol, acidity and sweetness as well as recognising aromas and discerning the wine's visual qualities. According to Bosker, a good blind tasting coach "can tell you if your acid calls are off base, how to distinguish a Sangiovese made in Montalcino from one made in Chianti and which floral scents are missing from your sense memory".

Candidates wanting to be an MS must first qualify as a Certified Sommelier, followed by achieving an Advanced Sommelier's Certificate, and finally, by invitation only, the Master Sommelier Diploma. Blind tasting is required in all three qualifications. For the final one, the Court does not divulge examination papers, which are a closely guarded secret. Instead candidates are given only "signposts" to possible questions before they face the exam. To pass, one must achieve at least 75 per cent in all three sections of the exam, but participants are only told if they have passed or failed each section of the test. If they have passed some of these but not others, they can carry these through and just retake what they have failed.

Passing the Master Sommelier exam is a passport to the elite world of wine connoisseurs, but most of the wine professionals who take the exam fail it. In the 45 years following the establishment of the title in 1969, only 230 people achieved the rank of Master Sommelier. Becoming an MS is the highest qualification a wine pro can achieve. According to Bosker: "In terms of difficulty and prestige, attaining it is the dining room equivalent of being made a US Navy Seal." Of the 200 people who take the exam annually, 95 per cent fail. "On average, in the years leading up to the test, Master candidates will taste more than 20,000 wines and study for 10,000 hours", says Bosker.

In March 2013 a woman reached the final round of the competition for the first time. This was wine expert Veronique Rivest. "If service was an art, the blind tasting looked downright magical" says Bosker. "She approached a table lined with four glasses, each filled with a few ounces of wine. . . She had just 180 seconds to zero in on the precise aromas and flavours that defined the wine, then correctly deduce what she was drinking."

A difficult task considering there are "more than 50 different countries that produce wine, nearly 200 drinkable wines, more than 340 distinct wine appellations in France alone and more than 5,000 types of grapes that can be blended in a virtually infinite number of ways" (Bosker). Nonetheless, "she was undaunted and rattled off the profile of a 2011 Chenin Blanc from Maharashtra, India, with the ease of someone giving directions to her house", says Bosker.

Despite the good repute in which Master Sommeliers are held, many decades ago sommeliers were often failed chefs who took up a job where "they performed with all the charm of the beasts of burden, for which they're named", according to Bosker. (The word "sommelier" comes from *sommie*r, Middle French for a pack horse).

But today's budding wine experts have been educated at top educational establishments and are following what to them is a calling. They practise their blind tasting in exclusive groups that meet at top restaurants such as

Eleven Maddison Park, known as EMP, in New York, regarded as the highest-level blind tasting group in the city.

Currently, the Court of Master Sommeliers operates in Europe, the UK and the US. It also has members in Canada, Chile, Japan and other countries. As well as working in the world's top restaurants, Master Sommeliers can also be found in less formal eateries.

In recent decades the wine industry has developed and grown dramatically, and the role of the profession of sommelier has become more important within it. Half a century ago, the sommelier, who was somewhat of a rarity, would be proficient in the knowledge of a few wines, such as Bordeaux, Burgundy and the occasional German Riesling.

Established in 1977, the Court of Master Sommeliers is the examining body for the three Sommelier qualifications, including the most challenging of them all, The Master Sommelier Diploma. The Diploma was introduced in 1969 under the auspices of the Vintners' Company, the Institute of Masters of Wine and other related organisations.

For those seeking the MS badge of honour, the "red pin", it is an obvious advantage to be employed on the floors of the world's best restaurants. Good sommeliers learn to develop intuition and measure their own success by the satisfaction of their customers rather than the size of the bill. However, working in the wine trade is also an option. Some work for distributors or in the retail trade, some act as wine consultants or independent wine educators.

With such few numbers, men and women in the MS trade are much in demand. They can effectively choose where they want to work. By going into the business world, the Master Sommelier can, according to wine expert Steve Heimoff, move away from the elite circles of other sommeliers and into networks of professionals and consumers, thereby "democratising the world of fine wine".

Professional Mourners

FAKE MOURNERS, TECHNICALLY KNOWN AS moirologists, are trained actors who play the part of grief-stricken friends of the deceased. This could be a suitable job for anyone who thinks that they can successfully play the part of a dead person's friend without upsetting the other people at the funeral.

This service is more popular in some countries than others. A company called "Rent a Mourner" was founded in 2011 in Braintree, Essex by entrepreneur Ian Robertson. Interviewed in 2013 he said that the inspiration for his business came from the market growth in China, but in Asian and Middle Eastern countries there is a tradition of wailing rather than the quieter, more sombre proceedings that we are used to in this country.

He explained that he offered a service to relatives of the deceased who want to swell the numbers at the funeral. Robertson achieved around 50 bookings during the company's first year, but also turned away 60 requests for attendance at funerals that were too far away for the professional mourners to travel to. Robertson said in 2013 that he planned to expand the geographical area served by his business. He acknowledged that the practice is unusual in the UK but predicted it would soon catch on. But he was to be disappointed because sadly the business is now defunct.

The staff at Rent a Mourner were willing to act as if they were genuinely sad at the passing of someone they did not actually know, for a small fee. Before attending the funeral, the mourners-for-hire were briefed with essential information about the deceased so that they could pass themselves off as a grieving friend or relative. They would agree a "story" with the client so that the other mourners were fooled into thinking they knew the deceased. It could be tricky for them to make sure they blended in well to the situation and did not say the wrong thing. For this reason, Robertson's staff would meet with the client beforehand and agree to play the part of someone who knew the deceased socially or professionally. Ian Robertson said Rent a Mourner's staff "will be informed of the deceased's background, achievements failures etc. so that they can converse with the other mourners with confidence".

It was reported in 2013 that a growing number of people were hiring out their services as professional mourners for a two-hour ceremony and would often weep alongside distraught relatives as well as talk to them. According to Robertson, although it was still a niche market, the business was growing, and he planned to expand. He explained that this was due to the increasing number of Middle Eastern and East Asian migrants coming to the UK for whom the practice is part of their culture. In these regions there is a long history of professional mourning and the funeral is more of a celebration of the deceased's life than a sad event.

As consumer expert Jasmine Birtles who has researched the subject is reported as saying in 2013: "Multi-cultural Britain is experiencing a cultural shift in the way its mourners say their final farewells." Birtles, who is the founder of personal finance site *MoneyMagpie.com*, added: "Hiring a stranger to weep at a funeral may seem strange, but it's a deep-seated tradition in the East." According to Birtles: "It is only a matter of time before it crosses over into mainstream culture". She added: "At the moment it's not the sort of thing that most people can treat as a career, but if it continues to increase in popularity, then crying on demand could soon become a highly prized skill".

Examples of professional mourning occur in the Bible in both the Old and New Testaments. The practice of having paid mourners is thought to have originated in China and the Middle East but is also thought to have occurred in ancient Egyptian and Roman civilisations. According to the magazine *Psychology Today*, in ancient Egypt "there were always two professional women mourners present at a burial, who were representatives the goddesses Isis and Nephtys. To be a mourner, the women could not have born children".

In Roman times, the better off the person was while living, the more extravagant the funeral. At the funerals of the wealthy, "professional mourners would make up a large part of the procession. They could not be members of the family and would be paid to go to the burial crying and wailing loudly, ripping out their hair, tearing their clothes and scratching their faces" according to *Psychology Today*. The more professional mourners that attended the funeral, the greater the status of the deceased. Historically, professional mourners were generally women because it was not socially acceptable for men to cry in public.

In China, professional mourners date back to about 100 BC and the practice was common throughout the dynastic reigns. It was banned under the Cultural Revolution as a superstitious practice but has since become popular again. One of the most prominent professional mourners in China today is Hu Xinglian, professionally known as Dingding Mao, well known for her wailing, dancing and singing. She works with her brother and offers to crawl towards the coffin to beg the deceased to come back home. Her performances have been described as theatrical. She now takes bookings from across her region.

Professional mourning also has a history in some African countries. In South Africa, for example, one can pay to have someone not only cry but threaten to jump into the grave, although this comes at an extra cost. Professional mourning is part of the extravagant tradition of Ghanaian funerals. In this country people spend as much on a funeral as they do on a wedding and it is better to have as many mourners as possible. For this reason, billboards are used to announce the funeral arrangements. Sometimes artistically designed coffins are used, shaped as something reminiscent of the deceased. Some funerals are exotic enough to include dancing pallbearers.

As Madam Awo Yaadonkoh, leader of the Kumasi Funeral Criers Association, explained to CNN, professional mourners can help relatives of the deceased raise money from other funeral-goers. Some people even make it a provision of their wills that the services of the association should be utilised. She added: "The way we professionally cry moves sympathisers to give out more money to the bereaved families. That's the main reason people contact us."

The association offers a variety of ways of dramatic crying to suit the requirements of the customer. The styles of crying include "crying with swag", which means with style and confidence, "deep wailing and shouting, crying and rolling on the ground, crying and walking at the funeral ground, highly emotional crying, basic crying, crying and vomiting", according to *odditycentral.com*.

British based professional mourners need to be ready to dress in black and fit into the sad and stressful situation of a more traditional British funeral and be able to talk without saying the wrong thing. To do this job one must be an accomplished actor as well as a good conversationalist. For this reason, a professional mourner never goes to a funeral alone, but two are always sent so they can help each other out in tricky situations. Apart from these qualities it is essential to be a good timekeeper and have the ability to stay calm and relaxed in a difficult situation, and to have a good enough memory to retain all the vital information about the deceased.

Modern day professional mourners are used for the same reasons they always have been. The number of attendees at a funeral can be taken as a sign of the worth and status of the deceased. Sometimes, though, in the case of elderly people, most of their friends and associates have already died. Another reason to use paid mourners is that the deceased has few living relatives or those that survive are too far away to attend.

In some cultures, wailing and crying are included in this practice, sometimes because the relatives of the deceased are uncomfortable about expressing emotions in this way. Whatever the reason for hiring a professional mourner, it is better to meet them beforehand so that they know what you expect of them.

Numismatists

THE TERM "NUMISMATIST" MAY NOT be familiar to most people, but a numismatist is someone who studies coins and, in many instances, collects them. Coins provide a valuable addition to the historic record dating back several millennia. Related fields of study include paper currency and tokens.

The word numismatics comes from the adjective numismatic meaning "of coins" and is derived from the French *numismatiques*, which is based on the Greek *nomisma*. Numismatic value is the value in excess of the denomination of the coin, known as the "collector value." Nowadays the term numismatist is often used to describe coin collectors generally. Sometimes the terms coin collectors and numismatists can be synonymous; sometimes they are not. A coin collector can be a numismatist who studies coins, or just a collector of coins.

Some coin collectors aim to complete sets or certain types of coins, such as commemorative coins, without paying attention to their date, country of origin and even denomination. They collect coins, often just for the pleasure of owning a collection.

Numismatists on the other hand are more interested in detailed information about the coins they collect and often the value of their collection. They usually know the age of a coin, the history behind it, the metal content and even the mint from which it originated. This detailed knowledge of coins makes a numismatist's approach more scientific. With modern coins information such as their age and country of issue can be discovered at a glance, since it is always embossed on the coins. Historically, coins did not always provide this information, so it sometimes takes a skilled and experienced numismatist to establish it. Knowing where a coin was found can be helpful, but coins can be found far from their place of origin. Numismatists can be coin dealers, historians and researchers who are interested specifically in coins or paper money.

Coin hoarders are also distinct from coin collectors. They often have no idea of the value of the coins in their collection and do not organise them in any particular way. Coin collectors usually start out as hobbyists who collect as a pastime. This is usually because they are interested in the history, artistic appeal or sentimental value of the coins they add to their collection. Coins of historical interest may be ancient Greek, Roman or Byzantine examples, where the collector is interested in the stories behind the coins. Coin collectors usually organise their collections according to type. Although they may have some idea of the value of coins in their collection, they are often less interested in this aspect of it.

Coin inheritors are people who inherit a coin collection and may take an interest in it, or not. If they are interested, they may add coins to the collection that they have acquired themselves. If they are not interested in it, they may sell it or donate it to a museum or other establishment.

In the field of numismatics, there are coin investors and coin dealers. Coin investors understand the coin market and seek to know when the right time is to buy a particular type of coin. They also understand the grading of coins and how to make their collection grow in value and to avoid fake currencies. To succeed in the business, "a coin investor must keep up to date with the trends in coin pricing and has to know a good number of reputable coin dealers", as the *Old Coins Collecting Guide* describes it. Such people are often called professional numismatists and must have a good knowledge of grading and validating coins for commercial purposes.

Professional coin dealer Bill Panitch tells me he has been in the job over 40 years. He describes it as sometimes "an eight day of the week job" but adds "as the famous adage goes. . . 'Find something you love to do and you'll never have to work a day in your life.'" However, he would not recommend the job to anyone who did not have a great passion for it, as well as a good eye for detail. He says the business has changed dramatically over the past 10-15 years and is not as “easy” as it used to be.

Commercial buyers are more interested in the metal or bullion content of coins and so pay particular attention to gold and silver coins. However, the melting down of coins to make jewellery or for other commercial purposes is actually illegal.

Numismatists often take a special interest in coins that were minted only for a short time or have minting errors, which makes them rarer. According to Panitch, these are often valuable but sometimes less so. Experts also seek out coins that are particularly beautiful or historically significant. The Royal Mint, for example, mints one-off commemorative coins such as gold sovereigns which celebrate events such as the Queen’s Sapphire Jubilee. These are designed to be much more valuable than the official face value of the coin.

Until the twentieth century, coins in general circulation were usually made from scarce metals such as gold and silver. This was because precious metals were generally accepted as having an intrinsic value and could be accepted as payment over a wide geographical area. Over time the transport of large quantities of valuable coins became too inconvenient and subject to loss, so paper money was introduced, but since this had no intrinsic value it was acceptable over a smaller geographical area.

Historically, coin collecting was known as the “hobby of kings” because only such people as secular and ecclesiastical rulers and dignitaries had the financial means and contacts to generate a large coin collection. It is thought that Caesar Augustus had an international coin collection, mostly consisting of gifts from rulers of foreign countries, given for diplomatic purposes and to facilitate trade agreements. Pope Boniface VIII also had a collection. The Italian scholar Petrarch is known as the first Renaissance collector and presented a collection to Emperor Charles IV of the Holy Roman Empire in 1355.

In the mid-1800s, coin collecting societies began to emerge. These included the Royal Numismatic Society which was founded in 1836 and immediately started to publish its journal that became the *Numismatic Chronicle.* This society is international in subject and membership. It provides research grants and prizes for numismatic study. The American Numismatics Society founded in New York City in 1858 began publishing the *American Journal of Numismatics* in 1866. There are other organisations dedicated to numismatics from which a numismatist may gain a lot of information about rare and collectible coins. There are also trade fairs where valuable knowledge can be obtained. Many books have been written on the subject as well.

The advent of the internet has meant that formerly local coin collecting clubs and societies now have a global reach. The internet can help collectors acquire coins from across the world and assist them with research work.

As well as the coins themselves, numismatists study their place in history of money. Analysis is sometimes used to determine the age of coins. As one source puts it: "Modern metal analysis provides clues as to the origin and fineness of the coinage metal used." This allows devaluation by the lowering of precious metal content to be established. This was done by rulers for such purposes as funding wars.

Another approach, known as "contextual numismatics" examines the geographical spread of finds of particular types of coins. This provides an insight into the trading relationships and routes of different communities. However, one of the challenges of this type of research is that only one in a thousand ancient coins issued is thought to have been discovered. Beside the coins themselves, written historical sources provide a valuable insight into the study of numismatics.

Numismatics is carried out by museums and universities across the globe and examples are kept from the earliest times of coin usage to the present day. From time to time new hoards or collections come into the possession of a museum or university which must be identified and classified. Universities consider numismatics to be a subsidiary subject to disciplines such as history and classical studies as well as archaeology. Knowledgeable collectors make their own contribution to the numismatic research done by museums and universities. Coins dating back to the seventh century BC survive in coin collections today and without them our knowledge of the past would be seriously diminished.

Orrery Making

SINCE PREHISTORIC TIMES, HUMANS HAVE been studying the sky at night, looking for patterns of predictability in the movements of the stars. From ancient times, astronomers have been monitoring the movement of the constellations and the planets using the Zodiac.

In antiquity people started using astrolabes and other devices to try to track the movement of the stars and the planets. These were the forerunners of the orrery which is a device designed to provide a model of the solar system which predicts the movement of the planets around the sun. An orrery is "a clockwork mechanism that simulates the motion of the planets (and in some cases their major moons) around the Sun", as described by *universetoday.com*. Most of these models were made after the acceptance of the fact that the planets travel in orbit around the Sun, known as heliocentric orbit, rather than the other way around.

The centre of an orrery is thus a representation of the sun with each of the planets at the end of an arm emanating out of the centre. It is usually too difficult to make these models to scale "partly because of the difficulty in mechanically modelling the distances involved, the eccentricity of various planets' orbits and the planets massive differences in terms of size", according to *universetoday.com*.

The Antikythera mechanism dates back to 159-100 BC and is thought to be the earliest orrery still in existence. It was discovered in a shipwreck off the Greek island of Antikythera in 1900 and consisted of a hand operated mechanism that represented the diurnal movements of the Sun, the Moon and the five planets that were known at the time. These were Mercury, Venus, Earth, Mars and Jupiter. It reflects the cosmological theories of the ancient Greeks and placed the Earth at the centre of the solar system. For many decades it was thought to be far too complex to be genuine and was not taken seriously as a historical artefact.

The Roman philosopher Cicero described a machine built by Archimedes around 200 BC that showed the relative positions of the Sun, the Moon and the Earth. Unfortunately, no other evidence of this device exists. With the fall of the Roman Empire and the onset of the dark ages, this learning was lost and would not return until the medieval period.

The first clockwork mechanism was built by Giovanni Dondi in 1348. This represented the elliptical orbits of the Sun, the Moon, Mercury, Venus, Mars, Jupiter and Saturn, which had by then been discovered. It placed the Earth at the centre of the Solar System, which was still believed to be the case at the time. Although the device itself is lost, Dondi left a detailed description of its mechanism.

The design of orreries changed with Copernicus's heliocentric model of the Solar System published in 1543, Newton's Law of Gravitation of 1687 and other scientific discoveries during the early modern period. This was a time known as the "Scientific Revolution". Acceptance of the heliocentric model of the solar system, with the Sun at the centre, meant that orbits were more easily represented as circular or elliptical orbits.

The first orrery of the modern kind was built by clock makers George Graham and Thomas Tompion in 1704. The name is derived from Charles Boyle, the fourth Earl of Orrery who, on hearing about Graham and Tompion's invention, commissioned instrument maker John Rowley to use their design to build one for himself.

An orrery exists in a planetarium built in Franeker in the Netherlands between 1774 and 1781 by Eise Eisinga, known as Eisinga's Planetarium. This contains an orrery which covers the room's ceiling. According to *universetoday.com*: "The clockwork machine that powers it has been in almost continuous operation since it was first opened." Most of the mechanical work goes on in the space above the ceiling. The planets' orbits are represented in real time.

Early orreries were built for scientific or educational establishments or for rich collectors and continued to grow in size and complexity. By the Victorian era cheaper models became available. With the increasing use of planetariums orreries became less popular and almost disappeared. The decline probably began in 1770 with Adam Walker's Eidouranion, a planetarium that used a projector. Once Carl Zeiss introduced his own version in 1924 the standard projector system still used today had been established and orreries became virtually redundant for a time.

As modern day orrery maker John Gleave told researcher Matthias Meir, "Why compete with nothing more than brass gears and wooden boxes against these fancy light shows?" But as Gleave put it: "Working as an artist and painter. . . the mechanical beauty and craftsmanship of these mechanisms appealed to me." Since he had always wanted to work with metal, he decided to build his own orrery. He found it difficult to adjust from working as an artist to working with gears and transmission, but he now seems to have mastered the technique quite successfully and has built around 170 of them. These range from simple Earth-Moon models to examples that include the moons of Saturn moving independently. On one occasion he built an orrery four feet (1.22 m) wide that was too large to get out of the door of the room in which he built it. "Ultimately I had to dismantle it," he said. He now prefers not to build such large examples.

Fellow orrery maker, Australian Brian Greig told Meir that a sensitivity to art, as well as an understanding of mechanical engineering, is necessary for the job. Beside this, he says "you need the patience of Job, the wisdom of Solomon, the strength of Sampson and a bank account the size of Rockefeller's." He offers traditional orreries as well as specialist models such as tellurians which represent the Earth's seasons, lunariums which are built to describe the complex motion of the moon and Jovians which represent the movements of Jupiter and its moons. Greig says it took him about three years to create his first machine.

Although the work of a clock maker is similar, most orreries are built by scientific instrument makers, such as Greig, who now produces three or four orreries in a year. As was the case with early models, most of them are built for scientific establishments or rich collectors. A basic model of the earth and the moon costs from approximately £3,000 at the time of writing. Despite the competition from planetaria and now computer software as well, orreries continue to be objects of fascination for most people who see them.

Apart from the models built by such people as Gleave and Grieg, known as solid models, there are two other types of orrery. These are real world orreries, usually of walking distance from the centre to the periphery and virtual orreries, which have almost limitless possibilities.

The largest real world orrery on the planet is based in British Columbia, Canada. In this case, according to *Universe Today*, the Sun is located in Star Park, Oak Bay, Victoria, while Pluto is located on the western side of Vancouver Island. Beyond this the furthest known object in our solar system, the Ort Cloud is thousands of kilometres away at the Canadian Embassy in Beijing, China. Many other "physical orreries" exist including the York Solar System Model Orrery built by York University. This one covers a radius of 6.4 miles (10.3 km). As well as all the planets this contains models of the Cassini and Voyager spacecraft, which are constantly on the move. At Armagh observatory in Northern Ireland, there is a human observatory where people can play the part of the planets. However, since it is built to scale, due to their immense distance, Uranus and Neptune could not be included.

Digital orreries are designed on a computer at a relatively low price, using modern technology. Examples include the one at the University of Texas and a Solar System Visualiser run by the University of Minnesota. There is also an example, built in 1985, at the Smithsonian Institute in Washington DC which is designed to answer long standing questions about the solar system.

From prehistoric times, humans have looked in wonder at the stars at night. Our understanding of the universe has come a long way since then. Not only have we built ever more complex machinery to study space, but we have experience of exploring it directly.

Pardoners

ACCORDING TO THE TEACHINGS OF the Roman Catholic Church, a pardon or indulgence was a means of reducing the time one spent in purgatory. In the early days of the church pardons were granted at the intercession of Christians about to be martyred or at least imprisoned, because of their faith. Later, pardoners, originally called "questors", were responsible for the pardoning of sins on behalf of the Roman Catholic church and were particularly prevalent during the Middle Ages.

Pardoners were supposed to show their letters of authority to a church congregation, charge money for the pardoning or indulgence of sins and prescribe a penance to each individual. This would often include the recitation of prayers, a visit to a pilgrimage site or other good works. The money was supposed to be sent to the bishop to help with charitable causes such as hospitals or relief of the poor. It was sometimes appropriated by Catholic rulers for expensive projects such as the crusades and the building of cathedrals. They also funded civil construction projects, including the building of roads and bridges.

According to *The Pardoner's Prologue and Tale Study Guide*: "Some [pardoners] were monks or priests, others were properly licensed lay people employed to perform this function." The practice was often farmed out to contractors who could be more or less reliable. As well as handing out penances to the congregation, they would inform them about the need for repentance, confession and the performance of penances. However, a pardoner could not hear confessions himself, which was the role of the priest. Indulgences were issued on the basis that parishioners confessed their sins as soon as possible. Some people did not realise they had to make a confession as well, and thought they were simply paying for the forgiveness of sins and performing a penance which they believed would reduce their time in purgatory. The article *Caxton's Chaucer – Pardoners and Indulgences* describes how "The recitation of specific prayers listed in the fifteenth century printed *Book of Hours* was stated to reduce the time one spent in purgatory by a few days or hundreds or even thousands of years."

The fake forgiveness of the unscrupulous pardoners was based not on penance but the payment of money which they kept for themselves. They had letters of indulgence which acted as receipts for forgiveness with a space for the purchaser's name at the bottom. With the invention of printing, thousands of indulgences could be produced daily from a single press. This was good for the pardoners, who could sell more indulgences, and for printers who found it a good way to make money. Caxton's first printed indulgence dates from 1476, about the time Chaucer published the first edition of his *Canterbury Tales*. It is not known how many indulgences were printed, but an institution based in London is known to have issued 30,000 indulgences a year. Only a few of these exist today.

Although pardoners were not supposed to preach, they often did. Yet they were known for their lax private lives and often made money on the side selling fake relics.

By exploiting parishioners' wishes to be repentant, corrupt pardoners could easily make much more money than could be achieved by honest work. All that was needed were some convincing fake letters, not much of a problem in an age when most people were illiterate. Simple congregations were easily taken in and would be easily fooled by the fake documents. They would not have realised that the money they paid was going to the pardoner's own pockets rather than to a good cause. This practice was widespread because it satisfied the parishioner's wish for easy repentance, and the pardoner's aim to make easy money.

Pardoners were also notorious for their lewd tales in church which amused the parishioners and led them to be more generous with money. As an academic commentary on Chaucer's Pardoner says: "Since 'the gentles' have listened with enjoyment already to the very ribald tales of the Miller and the Reeve, they must have been expecting something really objectionable from the Pardoner."

Given the prevalence of corrupt pardoners at the time, readers of Chaucer's Pardoner in the *Canterbury Tales* would not have been surprised that this individual was a conman. In this story, the pardoner goes through the pretence of absolving people's sins although he was not entitled to do so. Theologians argued that although this was a sin on the part of the pardoner, parishioners might be forgiven anyway because they did not realise the pardoner's deceit. Like all corrupt pardoners, Chaucer's is a con man who takes the money for himself. The pardoner exploited people's wish for forgiveness of their sins and traded on their feelings of guilt and fears of eternal damnation.

Pope Clement V, who reigned from 1305 to 1314, strongly opposed these malpractices and did a great deal to hold back the corrupt pardoners. It was relatively easy to control the official pardoners, but rogues abounded particularly in England, where there were more of them than in other parts of Europe.

In 1392, more than a century before Martin Luther published his theses, Pope Boniface IX condemned the excesses of some members of religious orders who claimed that they had the authority of the Pope to sell forgiveness without the need for repentance.

The practice of issuing indulgences was one of the main reasons for Luther's criticism of the Church which led to the Reformation. Eventually the Catholic Reformation tried to rein in the worst excesses of the malpractice. The Council of Trent, which met in 1562, reserved the role of pardoner to ordained priests, who would be paid nothing for the task. The publication of indulgences was to be the responsibility of the bishop of the diocese only. At the council's final session in December 1563 it was declared that "all evil gains for the obtaining of (pardons) would be wholly abolished" and instructed bishops to be on the lookout for any malpractices. A few years later, in 1567, Pope Pius V abolished all financial transactions for the awarding of indulgences.

Reforms in the twentieth century abolished the quantification of indulgences which meant that they no longer represented a time period which would otherwise be spent in purgatory. The reforms also meant that the number of indulgences granted for pilgrimage to holy sites was seriously diminished.

While the work of a pardoner who takes money for indulgences is in itself controversial, the fact that, as Chaucer attests, many of them were corrupt and took the money for themselves, makes the practice even more so. However, over time the excesses of corrupt pardoners were reined in and the selling of indulgences has long been prohibited by the Catholic Church.

Peruke Making

THE WEARING OF WIGS OR perukes dates back to antiquity. In ancient Egypt they were a sign of status and were supposed to make their wearers look more dignified. In the Roman era dress was often not an indication of a woman's status, so women of the elite class flaunted their wealth with the wearing of expensive and elaborate wigs. The more complex the style of the wig, the greater the status of the woman wearing it. Those who could not afford these complex wigs, instead piled up their hair with wires, dyed it, created intricate curls and adorned it with flowers, jewels and pearls.

Many women imitated Queen Elizabeth I who wore red coloured wigs, thought to come from the hair of horses and perhaps even children. Wigs became popular for women in the late sixteenth century, having been introduced to England around 1572.

In the seventeenth century it became fashionable for European and colonial men and women of the elite class to wear wigs known as perukes. Louis XIV of France started this fashion by wearing them when he began to lose his hair at the age of seventeen, around 1655, probably due to syphilis. He hired 48 wigmakers to provide him with a great selection of perukes. By 1660 there were around 200 wigmakers providing their services to the French court. Louis XIV took to wearing yellow perukes and this became a fashion there. Between 1723 and1756 there were at least 1,200 wig shops in Paris which together employed around 6,000 wigmakers.

After the English Civil War (1642-1651) the new puritanical authorities of Cromwell's Commonwealth took power. This period of abstinence came to an end with the restoration of the monarchy in 1660, when Charles II took the throne. His use of flamboyant wigs, following the French fashion, encouraged imitation by his wealthier subjects.

The seventeenth and eighteenth centuries were an era of sophistication and affectation in dress and appearance when wigs made from human hair became obligatory for upper class men and women. The less well-off often followed suit by wearing wigs made from horse-hair, goat hair, wool or cotton. Human hair is thought to have come from monks whose heads had been shaved, peasant girls from Germany, Italy and France who did not mind losing their hair because they wore traditional headdresses, people in need of extra cash and inmates of prisons and workhouses.

However, at the time rumours abounded that the hair in fact came from street sweepings, or even plague victims, as was commented on by Samuel Pepys in his diaries in 1665. Pepys had a peruke made from his own hair in 1663. Since they were unsure of the origin of the materials they were using, more responsible peruke makers would often boil them in nitric acid or bake them to cleanse them of vermin, parasites and nits.

During this period upper class gentlemen paid great attention to their wigs. For women the fashion was more for partial wigs, hair extensions and hair lifting to produce outlandish coiffures, which could be up four feet high and matted with lard, and so prone to attract the attention of mice and insects.

From 1600 to 1800 wigs came in a variety of styles and natural colours including golden, reddish, brown and white. Powder was also applied to achieve the preferred colour. Originally wigs were manufactured by barbers, but during the seventeenth and eighteenth centuries the demand for complicated and elaborate wigs required the work of craftsmen skilled in this trade. These people, known as peruke makers or wig makers, were organised into guilds during the 1600s. The first wigmakers' guild was established in France in 1665 as wigs became popular both there in Britain.

These guilds provided training opportunities that involved an exam. Professional peruke makers hand crafted their wigs and carried out maintenance on existing ones including, cleaning, repair, refreshment of the curls as well as powdering and scenting the wigs. The industry provided jobs for many people particularly in England and France.

It is often assumed that in the seventeenth and eighteenth centuries wigs were worn only by the elite class and were a "display of power and status", according to the historical novelist Lucinda Brant. Indeed, Louis XIV required the hair of ten persons to create one copious wig with an excessive profusion of flowing locks. Yet by the end of his reign, the wearing of wigs had spread to all classes. so much so that by the mid-1700s wig wearing was adopted by tutors, cooks, messengers, shopkeepers and servants. Many of these men owned two wigs, one for everyday use and one for Sunday best. According to Lucinda Brant, "The wig was such a universal object of consumption that it became synonymous not with luxury but with convenience."

Eighteenth century men wore wigs for both formal and informal occasions. From 1700 the shorter "bob wig" was used by men of all classes for everyday wear. Longer, voluminous wigs were worn for special occasions until around 1730. After that the style became shorter. By the mid-1700s, wealthy gentlemen generally wore white coloured wigs, which were the most expensive. For those who could afford it, naturally white hair was used, while those who could not, used white or grey hair powder or made do with the cheaper coloured wigs of chestnut or brown. These were powdered and brushed back from the forehead and tied at the back with a black ribbon known as the Solitaire, which originated in France. By the 1780s fashionable young men would powder their own natural hair instead of wearing a wig. Powder was originally applied mainly as a degreaser but later came to be used as a colouring agent, where white was a popular colour. This method was preferred to the use of dyes which were affected by water.

Wigs made from new materials attracted the more eccentric customer or the "dandy". Horace Walpole, the son of Britain's first prime minister, wrote a letter dated 1751 about the odd manner of dressing of a fellow aristocrat, Edward Wortley Montagu, stating: "The most curious part of his dress, which he has brought from Paris, is an iron wig, you literally would not know it from hair."

During the eighteenth century the fashion for women was to adorn their hair with ribbons, jewels, flowers and even stuffed animals. The "a la fregate" style was introduced to fashionable society with its "model warship riding on rippling wavers of hair", as the Chertsey Museum puts it. Ladies of the elite class hired professional hairdressers to style their hair and add false locks to enhance their appearance. Fashionable ladies "were expected to augment their own hair with false hair, padding, powder, wires and ornaments" (Chertsey Museum). Powdering was used to colour the hair and colours included violet, blue, pink and yellow.

Hair powdering whether for perukes or natural hair was a messy task. Special rooms or wig closets were set up in the homes of the well-to-do. To avoid the necessity to attend to the hairstyle every day, women would often wear taffeta night caps

After 1790 wigs and hair powder became the preserve of older gentlemen of more conservative tastes. In 1795, the English government, in a programme to impose taxes on luxury goods, placed a levy on hair powder. This finally ended the fashion for peruke wearing by Englishmen by 1800. In France the association of wigs with the aristocracy, who had originally adopted the fashion, meant that the fashion for wearing them disappeared during the Terror in 1793.

Wigs were generally not durable, and few examples exist today. Our knowledge of them is almost entirely drawn from paintings, drawings, engravings and sculpture as well as written accounts. Various styles of wig can be seen in the works of Hogarth and other contemporary artists. As fashions came and went, older people continued to wear wigs that had gone out of fashion, and in the legal profession, wigs became part of their traditional costume and are still worn today.

Pet Food Tasting

IT MIGHT SEEM THAT ANYONE who is willing to taste-test pet food must be a little odd, but it is a highly skilled job. More time is spent doing research than tasting pet food. The taster's main job is testing the food for nutritional value and finding ways to improve the foods being developed. However, the job does also involve tasting the food.

Obviously pet food manufacturers want pets to enjoy their food as much as possible, but since the animals cannot speak for themselves, human pet food tasters are often employed to assess the smell, flavour and texture of their products. If they find them objectionable, the pets probably will too. Since much research has been done, human tasters have a pretty good idea of what cats and dogs like to eat.

Cats and dogs have different preferences. As Ness Bird of Arden Grange Pet Foods tells me, it is much more difficult to create a palatable cat food than dog food since cats, as natural hunters, are more discerning than dogs who are scavengers in their natural habitat. She says both dogs and cats can taste meaty, sour and bitter flavours, but dogs can taste sweet and salty flavours, while cats cannot. Bird adds that cat taste receptors are finely attuned to acidic and bitter stimuli, which helps them avoid ingesting toxic foods, but this makes it more difficult to create a palatable cat food because cats will identify foods as bitter or acidic when dogs or humans will not. Arden Grange do not employ anyone specifically as a pet food taster but allow their employees to volunteer during the development stage.

The smell of the food is crucial to this as animals experience it much more powerfully than humans. Also, the taster must bear in mind that when customers dislike the smell of a pet food themselves, they are less likely to buy it.

Although taste and smell are important, nutrition is the key to healthy pets and much of the pet food taster's job often involves creating improved new recipes with greater nutritional value.

Some pet food manufacturers go to the trouble of meeting the standards of nutrition and production that are applied to food intended for human consumption. In any case the meat used must be passed as fit for human consumption under the Animal Feed Regulations 2010. Much of it, however, is not designed with the nutritional needs of humans in mind, and so is not suitable for humans to eat.

The job of pet food taster does not require any specific skills apart from a willingness to consume food intended for animals and a sense of what pets prefer to eat. However, having certain traits makes the job much easier. These include being methodical and good at observing details, as well as the ability to give honest, constructive feedback about the latest style of pet food before it hits the market.

One also needs to be comfortable with putting pet food in one's mouth and chewing it for a considerable time. Like human food tasters, those of the pet food variety do not actually swallow the food but spit it out instead. However, they must chew it for long enough to identify the ingredients and suggest any changes that may improve the product.

Employers seek out candidates with experience in food preparation, such as catering, which requires people to have a good palate. Although it is "just pet food", the taster must be able to discern flavours, in the same way as an experienced wine taster does. The job also involves writing reports that are analytical in describing the subtleties of flavour and texture, so an analytical and methodical approach with good use of the English language is helpful. These reports also describe the nutritional content of the food and pet food tasters are always looking to suggest new formulas, production methods and packaging, to make the product as attractive as possible to both owner and pet.

A temporary job as a pet food taster is often a good way for students to earn some extra money. Jobs of this kind are not generally advertised publicly but are available to those who wish to track them down. A lot of the entry level jobs are temporary or part-time, with companies recruiting to test a new product. The range of different jobs goes from "the lowly Quality Assurance Assistant, regularly tasting the entire range of foods to check for consistency and make general flavour notes, all the way to the experienced Technical Director who is also responsible for creating new recipes as well as giving regulatory and technical advice to the business", to quote *myjobhub.com*.

Food tasters must repeatedly test samples of food and spit it out before moving on to the next one, all the while making notes and reports, carrying out a scientific study of the products in a laboratory. This work is very repetitive and comprises most of the role of the quality assurance assistant. The food "will be checked for around 40 taste reference points such as woodiness, smokiness and meatiness. Reference points for smell, appearance and texture are also used." (*myjobhub.com*).

Another route for getting into work as a pet food taster is as a food technologist. For this a degree in food science or nutrition is a suitable qualification. Alternatively, on the job training can suffice, working as a lab technician. There is currently a shortage of food technologists in the UK so there are plenty of jobs available. At the time of writing a food technologist can earn anything from £20,000 for a new recruit to £50,000 for an experienced technical director.

One of the best-known pet food tasters in the world is Simon Allison, who has made a name for himself as an honest and reputable taster who has the best of intentions for both pets and their owners. The first pet food he tasted was a turkey and cranberry dinner in 2006. He worked for Marks & Spencer with the aim of coming up with "the ultimate in feline and canine cuisine" (*mirror.com*), where he was responsible for the company's luxury range. His favourite recipe there was organic chicken with vegetables which he fed to his own three cats. He was concerned not only with taste and aroma but palate texture as well. Preferably it should be spreadable on bread almost like paté, he said.

Even Allison refrained from swallowing the food. "I'd be quite a different shape", he explained to *Mirror Online* in 2008. He also guarded against bad breath odour by washing his mouth out after every tasting session and by chewing gum. Nonetheless "I love my job", he said, "It's just the same as if I worked for the ready meals department." He pointed out that most pet owners like to give them food similar to that they would like themselves. As he puts it: "The more we make pet food like the owner's food, the more comfortable we think customers will be serving it."

Another expert in this field is Philip Wells, who tasted dog food for a living. He was until recently Technical Director at Lily's Kitchen. He is quoted as saying he liked the Lovely Lamb with Peas and Parsley best. "Dogs' palates are different from humans' ", he said, "but taste is an important quality check to ensure each different ingredient is perfectly balanced in just the right proportions."

Wells explained that he tasted each batch of each recipe of dog food and did so every day. He didn't just get stuck into the food straightaway. His first step was to look at it to see if it had the right mix of ingredients and then he gave it a good sniff. He explained that pet food sold by his company used only freshly prepared produce, so the dog food he tasted didn't smell like "normal pet food." He also tasted food from other companies as part of his market research. "There are some pretty gruesome pet foods out there" he added.

Pet food tasters not only feed their pet food to cats and dogs but quite literally try it for themselves. "And for what it's worth, I quite like it." said Wells. He said he "pretty much" enjoyed the job, and found it rewarding because it helped pets become happier and healthier. But most of all he enjoyed working with "a key member" of the tasting team, Lilly the border terrier.

Most of the pet food companies that employ human tasters produce premium quality products, which are suitable for human consumption and often taste good, not just to animals, but to humans as well.

Phrenology

PHRENOLOGY WAS A PSEUDO-SCIENTIFIC PRACTICE which was carried out mostly in the nineteenth century with the intention of trying to determine people's personality, based on the contours of their skulls. Its proponents called it "the only true science of the mind." The idea was originally proposed by the Viennese physician Franz Joseph Gall (1758-1828).

His theory was based on the idea that the brain is composed of multiple, distinct, innate capacities. Because these capacities are distinct, it follows that each faculty of a person's personality must be located in a separate part of the brain. Gall proposed that the brain consisted of multiple areas or "organs", each responsible for a different aspect of one's personality. He believed that the shape of each particular organ determined its power and that the shape of the brain as a whole reflected this. The theory also applied to animals who were thought to have fewer brain "organs". Those that are common to both humans and animals were, for example, those concerned with "love of one's offspring", "memory" and "the instinct for self-defence", while those related to "a sense of satire" and "a sense of metaphysics" were only to be found in humans, says science website *The Big Picture*.

Since the skull takes its shape from that of the brain, he argued, the shape of the skull can be used to determine personality traits, good or bad. He believed an examination of the contours of the skull provided an indication of a person's aptitudes and tendencies by revealing the development of each particular organ. To give an example, "a prominent protuberance in the forehead at the position attributed to the organ of benevolence" would indicate a kind personality. (*historyofphrenology.org.uk*).

But Gall and his fellow phrenologists sought only for evidence that confirmed their theories and ignored evidence that contradicted them. Any evidence which they thought confirmed their beliefs was quickly publicised by them as "proof" that their ideas were true. Meanwhile cases of people who were not very benevolent but had an enlarged area of the brain thought to be responsible for this characteristic, were ignored. Gall defended his methods by saying: "As the skull takes its shape from the brain, the surface of the skull can be read as an accurate index of psychological aptitudes and tendencies."

The history of phrenology dates back to the 1790s when Gall and his protégé J.G. Spurzheim, both Germans, founded the "science". In 1815 phrenology received a damning critique in the respected publication, the *Edinburgh Review*. However, this notoriety brought phrenology to the attention of the general public when it had previously only been discussed in medical circles.

Spurzheim refuted his critic in the *Edinburgh Review*, an act which won him many converts in Edinburgh.

It was here the first Phrenological Society was founded in 1820, followed by many others in both Britain and the US over the next few decades. These included the British Phrenological Society founded by well-known phrenologist L.N. Fowler in 1887, whose name can sometimes be found embossed on a phrenological bust in antique shops or on psychologists' desks. Members of the society not only practised phrenology but published phrenological journals as well, which tried to emulate scientific journals of the time. The Phrenological Association was founded in Newcastle, England, in 1838 and was designed to imitate the British Association for the Advancement of Science, from which phrenology had been excluded since it was not accepted by mainstream science.

Early phrenologists were often political and social reformers and, in some cases, ultra-radicals. Indeed, many historians associate phrenology with reformist and radical ideas. Some evangelicals were also followers of phrenology because they believed it was evidence of God's work. Most phrenologists were, however, much more secular. Many in the church rejected phrenology because it suggested that the mind was in the brain rather than the soul.

More responsible phrenologists were aware of the great authority they had in "scientifically" determining a person's personality, which according to the *historyofphrenology.org.uk* "they claimed could not be matched by any other 'science"'.

Phrenology spread from Britain to France and the US in the 1830s and 1840s and was later revived in Germany. When it reached America, it became very fashionable. During the 1860s and 1870s a phrenological movement led by the "Phrenological Fowlers", namely L.N Fowler and his brother O.S. Fowler, spread from the US back to Britain. Their theories were based on Gall's system. When they came to Britain, they pursued a successful lecture tour of the country and went on to set up phrenological institutions, societies and publishing houses. By now phrenology was less "science"-based and more entrepreneurial in nature.

Phrenology began as an interest of the cultural and scientific elite before becoming a popular middle-class phenomenon, through phrenological societies, and finally descended into a disreputable practice carried out by so called "professors of phrenology", who read heads for profit. A document was published by one of these, H. Lundie, titled *The Phrenological Mirror*. This included advice on pricing for the service, the role of each organ and its size and the four classical humours or temperaments, which phrenology had taken on board.

In order to carry out their examination, phrenologists would run their fingers or, as Gall recommended, the palms of their hands, over the skull to identify any elevations or indentations. Some also used callipers, measuring tape and other instruments. The first thing they did was to establish the overall shape of the skull to get an overview of the person's temperament and character. Skilled phrenologists would be familiar with Gall's map of the skull, adapted according to the latest phrenological charts, but also the "organs" of the brain and the role of each of these in determining the patient's personality. The number of organs that were believed to exist gradually increased over time.

During the peak of phrenology's popularity in the 1830s-1840s, employers could demand a phrenological report to serve as a character reference for a prospective employee to check whether they were honest and hard working. The theories of phrenology were also applied to education and criminal reform. However, it was rarely used in a court of law.

Phrenology was a popular way of deciding on a suitable career for a young person and as a "scientific" way to find a suitable partner. Gullible people were easily taken in.

As a science, phrenology has been almost completely discredited since the mid-nineteenth century. Even at the height of its popularity it was much disputed, especially by members of the scientific community. It was never given the status of an accredited science which its most ardent advocates, such as George Combe, an Edinburgh lawyer, and his brother Andrew, dearly wished for.

Cranial examinations were also used by racial anthropologists during the late nineteenth and early twentieth centuries to try to vindicate the idea that Europeans were superior to other races. It was also used as a form of social Darwinism, placing one class below another. The Nazis used it as what they believed was "scientific" evidence of the superiority of the Aryan race.

Ironically, the theory that the functions of the brain are localised is now widely accepted. It is also true that areas of the brain more frequently used can become enlarged, such as "the right hippocampus of London taxi drivers", as described by the *historyofphrenology.org.uk.* Modern brain imaging techniques such as Functional Magnetic Resonance Imaging (FMRI), have been used to prove that the different areas of the brain relate to different functions. However almost all the regions of the brain described by Gall have been completely disproven.

Phrenology, although a popular craze in its heyday, was always considered by many scientists to be a "pseudo-science" which could result in possibly dangerous consequences. This was particularly true when it was used to determine character, honesty and criminal tendencies. Although the basic premise of phrenology, that different areas of the brain were responsible for different characteristics has been scientifically validated, a person's personality is not an innate quality.

Pit Brow Lasses

FOLLOWING A DISASTER AT THE Huskar Colliery near Barnsley in 1842 in which 26 children were killed, the British Government, led by Sir Robert Peel, put an end to the employment of women and young children underground. Before the Mines Act of 1842 made it illegal for women and girls to work underground, they could often be found working as drawers pulling carts in the mines, a practice known as "thrutching", which was a job that men were not keen to do. It involved crawling along like a flat-footed animal on one's hands and feet. The distances travelled in this way were seen by many philanthropists as excessive. The 1842 Act also made it illegal for boys under 10 to work underground.

There were a particularly large number of women working in the Lancashire mines. When the new law was introduced, some women mineworkers would dress in men's clothes and pit managers would turn a blind eye. It was not for another eight years that the first Inspector of Mines was appointed so this practice was largely left unchecked. While most British mines employed an exclusively male workforce, in Lancashire and some other areas there was a tradition of employing women mineworkers. These included South Staffordshire, Shropshire, South Wales and Scotland.

The tasks available to women above ground could be just as dangerous but earned them only a quarter of what the men working underground were earning. Women who worked on the surface of the mines were known as brow girls or "pit brow lasses" in the county of Lancashire. Their work involved "emptying the coal tubs, loading coal on to wagons, screening the coal to remove any impurities such as stones or dirt, and working in saw-mills which provided timber to be used as props in the mines" (*lighshawmeadows.com)*. They did not get the chance to rise above these badly paid jobs.

The Mines Act separated families who had worked together in the pits. With less income coming in, families found it harder to survive. Many women were willing to continue to work illegally even with a substantial pay cut.

With the new law coming into force, women drawing carts were replaced by pit ponies. Mine owners preferred to employ women since the upkeep of the ponies was more expensive than women doing the same job and the roofs of the mines had to be raised to accommodate the animals.

The penalty paid by mine owners for continuing to employ women underground was £10 per worker, which was not much of a deterrent especially as there were few inspectors to enforce it. Some mine owners compelled the women to pay the fine out of their own pockets, but in any case, the Home Office was often unwilling to pursue lengthy and costly trials.

Nonetheless women gradually moved into jobs on the surface of the mines. They were preferred by employers for these jobs because they worked for lower wages than men and had no union which could make trouble. Women began to replace men at picking tables, sorting the coal from the impurities.

The sorters would stand at the sorting tables sifting through the coal for stones and dirt. The poorer the quality of the coal, the more impurities there would be and hence a greater number of sifters would be employed. Widows of men who perished down the mines were usually given a place at the sorting tables, so that they could feed their families. Elderly and disabled male former miners were also involved in the coal sorting but were paid more than twice as much as women for doing the same job.

The women were scorned by many members of the public for wearing trousers and men's jackets and were criticised for their "lack of femininity". They were also an object of fascination to some, including the Victorian poet and eccentric Arthur Munby (1828-1910). Munby was fascinated by the size and strength of these "amazons" who carted huge coal tubs around the surface of the mines.

They can be seen photographed in picture postcards from the early twentieth century, but by then the wearing of trousers had mostly been replaced by a long rough skirt worn over leggings. It was necessary for them to wear suitable clothing for the long days they spent working in dirty conditions. They wore headscarves to prevent coal dust getting into their hair, but still found it stuck to their clothes and skin. Nevertheless, many women preferred this outdoor work to the alternatives available working in the noisy textile mills.

Most "pit brow lasses" were in their twenties. A few would go on working for much longer and one woman in Wigan went on into her sixties. They were legally required to be at least fifteen and "had parents, brothers or husbands also working in the mines. In fact, 99 per cent of them married miners", according to an article published by the National Mining Museum titled "Women in Mining Communities". Nonetheless they were a close-knit community which stood together in the face of the male-dominated industry.

Mine workers of all types typically worked six days a week, in 12 hour shifts on Monday to Friday and on Saturday their hours were reduced. However, there are known cases of women working up to 18 hours a day. With all the housework to do as well, there was little time left for leisure activities. Nevertheless, they would meet friends at the market days and dances were organised within the community as well as festivals to mark special occasions. At these events women took part in competitions such as baking contests. On Sundays, their only day off in the week, they would take turns to host tea parties for their friends from the mine.

Throughout the nineteenth century, the miners' union representing their male colleagues pressed for the replacement of female coal-pickers with disabled and retired male miners, which resulted in many of the women losing their jobs. The union believed that this would force up wages with which miners could support their families.

The pit brow women put up a spirited fight against attempts to introduce new laws to ban them from colliery work. These included two attempts to introduce legislation in 1887 and 1911. On both occasions women from Wigan travelled to Parliament to protest, sending a deputation to the Home Secretary. There were unlikely scenes of the women in their working clothes visiting the Palace of Westminster. They were successful in their efforts to prevent these laws being passed.

Some well-meaning philanthropists believed the work at the pit head was too arduous for women, even if they were physically strong, and that only lads should be employed to work at the mines. Nonetheless, the work was less dangerous than factory work and no more laborious than agricultural work, in which many women were employed.

As technology developed during the early twentieth century automated machinery took over the role of coal pickers in general. By mid-century, there were only 1,000 women left working in this role, whilst in 1841 there had been well over 5,000 women employed at the mines, many of them working as coal pickers. The last two women involved in mining retired in 1972 from a mine in Lowca on the Cumbrian coast, bringing to an end the employment of women in the mines. One of them, Rita Culshaw, told the *Daily Mirror* that she loved her work and would willingly return to it even at the age of 83.

Professional Queuing

FOR MOST PEOPLE QUEUING IS something they do not want to have to do, a boring task that takes time out of a busy day. Although queuing occurs in many countries, it is generally seen as a typically British custom. In some countries it hardly occurs at all.

For some people, though, queuing is a paid occupation rather than a waste of time which in many cases pays between £10 and £20 per hour. Experience or specific skills are not required. but sometimes one is entrusted with personal documents, for example when queueing for some bank, travel or medical purposes. Taking enough jobs to make queuing into a full-time job does require good time management skills. No qualifications are needed but the University of Sussex is reported to have offered a module in "The Theory and Practice of Remaining Motionless for Extended Periods of Time".

The job of traditional queuer originated in the USA. Professional queuers are employed by those who do not have the time to wait in line. Sometimes people will advertise on platforms such as Gumtree for someone to queue up and wait for them for a new iPhone or other sought-after product. Other people advertise their services as professional queuers. One such example was a student, Sabrina Sayed, who sat in the queue for every day of the Wimbledon Championships a few years ago, after arriving at five in the morning, to give up her place to her customer once the tickets went on sale. She held a silent auction, by text, the evening before the queues with the winner usually paying about £50 for her services. Three of her university friends followed suit. She admitted they sometimes get "dirty looks" from other queuers when they give away their places.

Another example is a student who queued for days for new fashion items such as the latest in Nike trainers which at the time cost him £180, to sell them on for £5,000. The market for professional queuers can be quite lucrative for this type of fashion event. Queues for the latest iPhone start days before its release and new designer trainers can entail queues that last a fortnight. Those who can afford it will happily pay to make sure they get a new product rather than waiting on the pavement for weeks. This can be done on their behalf by people who have plenty of free time and a lot of patience.

Black Friday sales events are also good for business. A hotel chain (RBH) has launched a guest package that includes an overnight stay at some of its UK hotels and the services of a professional queuer. Whilst the customers sit comfortably in their hotels, the shopper braves the wintery conditions overnight on their behalf. In the morning the customers are whisked away by taxi to arrive at the store "fresh, dry and ready to shop" (*incentivetravel.co.uk).* As Yvonne Brennan, group marketing manager put it in *incentivetravel.co.uk*: "Our Black Friday packages will allow guests to take advantage of this year's super discounts but without the stress of that quintessentially British pastime -- queueing."

The service is popular with serious Black Friday shoppers, including those looking for bargains and gifts and those looking for a spot of retail therapy. It is clear that there is plenty of business potential in professional queueing with the hype that retailers create around the latest goods they are launching.

In this endeavour, they partnered with professional queueing business Line Sitters, which has years of experience waiting in line for the latest fashions and technology. As Hasan Bux, General Manager of this company put it: "We have had great success in the past, getting hold of the newest, must-have gadgets and fashion items" (*incentivetravel.co.uk*).

In 2001 professional queuing agency Q4U was launched and charged £20 per hour for its services employing queuers, aged 20-50, operating in the London area. "It's a job that doesn't require a lot of skill or experience;

all you need is plenty of patience", Patrick Young, Director of 15 Minutes, the company that established the service, told *telegraph.co.uk*. "We're there for anything that involves queuing" he added. This can be for "travel documents, tickets, housing transactions, auctions or anything where people have to wait."

The queuers wait in line and then ring the business or individual when their turn is approaching or carry out the transaction for them. The business was kick-started when John Fashanu, the TV presenter and former footballer, paid a tramp £300 to buy him a £1 million flat. Fashanu hired the man to queue for two days before returning to buy the Kensington property.

Andrew Beck, another 15 Minutes director, told the *telegraph.co.uk*: "This is an idea which has become very popular in the Far East. In China, where you must queue for everything, professional queuers make more money than civil servants." A quick perusal of classified adverts in the Shanghai press reveals about 20 different agencies each employing up to 30 people. A burgeoning number of city dwellers in China has overwhelmed services such as banking and healthcare in metropolitan areas. The New Year exodus by migrant workers from the cities to their home villages creates a huge demand for train services. This is the world's largest human migration, totalling some 130 million people, which provides professional queuers with an opportunity to get work queuing for tickets, which takes a very long time. In China these people are known as "paotui" which means "running legs". Sometimes they get unusual requests like being employed by a retailer to queue outside their shop to make it look popular.

A South African professional queuer told the *Financial Times*: "Bureaucracy can be an overwhelming and long drawn out experience, especially in South Africa, so I am employed to queue at places such as the passport office in Johannesburg on behalf of people who need new ones." If people are submitting forms, the passport office makes sure all the documentation is correct before handing it back to the queuer. If the applicant needs to appear in person, the queuing agency transports them to the passport office to take the place of the professional.

It's a service for busy people who don't have the time to spend hours in line, queueing for whatever they need. As *myjobhub.com* puts it "What you are actually queuing for could be for anything, it doesn't really matter, the job is always the same".

Ravenmaster

THERE IS A FABLE ABOUT the Tower of London which states that during the seventeenth century King Charles II decreed that there should always be six ravens at the Tower. If there are none of them there, the story goes, the Kingdom of England will fall. In the 1940s when Hitler was trying to bomb Britain into submission and on the verge of invading it, the Tower was down to one raven, which begs the question, what would have happened if there had been none at all!

Since the 1950s, the flock of ravens, also known as an "unkindness" or a "conspiracy", have been looked after by an official Ravenmaster at the tower, who is responsible for maintaining the tradition of the birds' presence there. This person is chosen from one of the Yeoman Warders, the traditional guards of the Tower, who must have 22 years' exemplary military service and have achieved the rank of at least a warrant officer, to be appointed.

The incumbent Ravenmaster is Christopher Skaife, who has three assistants who cover for him on his days off. "I used to think my military career came to an end when I left the army", Skaife writes in his book: *The Ravenmaster, My Life with the Ravens at the Tower of London*, "but now I see that it was merely my apprenticeship."

His work with the ravens starts at first light when he greets them by name and releases them from the cages where they spend the night. The birds flutter out, before returning to their territories around the tower's greens, hours before the first visitors arrive. The next step for Skaife is to check that the birds are OK, feed and water them and clean out their cages. All this must be done before he has his own breakfast.

The birds are fed on raw meat, which mainly consists of chicken and mouse. As well as this they get nuts, berries, fruit and blood-soaked biscuits. They sometimes find food for themselves too. Skaife has seen one kill a pigeon in three minutes. Apart from this they get food given to them by visitors who are not supposed to feed them, especially as they may bite if they sense their territory is under threat.

During the day Skaife looks after the birds whilst carrying out his other duties as a one of the Tower's 35 Yeoman Warders, known as Beefeaters. As a member of the Tower's staff, Skaife lives within the walls of the Tower in a tradition that goes back 700 years. Originally, he lived in an apartment near the "Bloody Tower" but had to move elsewhere in the grounds because his first residence, where he believed things inexplicably moved around, was "too haunted". Skaife says he does not really believe in ghosts, but he does think that there are what he calls "echoes of the past" (*mentalfloss.com*).

The birds are free to roam around the Tower from dawn to dusk, sometimes crossing the Thames before coming back home when they return overnight to their cages, designed to protect them against foxes and feral cats. Open air cages are used at Skaife's insistence. The ravens' quarters are situated next to Wakefield Tower. Since he provides for their needs, the ravens see their master as the boss and generally return willingly to their enclosures at night. He whistles a distinctive tune to call them to bed. Nonetheless the Ravenmaster tries to prevent them from becoming too tame, since they are basically wild birds.

One day in mid -April 2019 Skaife noticed that two of the ravens, female Muninn and male Huginn, who joined the group towards the end of 2018, had built a large nest on which Muninn was sitting. Within two weeks four chirping chicks had arrived, the first to be hatched at the Tower since 1989. One of these will stay at the Tower and has been named George since the day of hatching was 23 April, which is St George's Day. There are currently seven other ravens at the Tower, the statutory six plus one spare. Their names are Harris (male), Poppy (female), Rocky (male), Grip (male),

Jubilee (male), Erin (female) and Georgie (male) Most come from breeders in Somerset, but Georgie was hatched at the tower.

In order to look after these birds in the height of summer, when the days are at their longest, Skaife must start his days at 4.30 am and end them as late as 9.30 pm. This leaves him with little free time. The birds are dangerous, too, with talons that could easily take his eye out, as well as sharp beaks. When examining them Skaife wears protective gear including a full-face mask and a gauntlet. Whilst feeding the birds he wears plastic gloves and takes a regular tetanus jab to protect himself against cuts or scratches. He has several scars on his arms which he has received from the birds.

Despite these downsides, Skaife enjoys caring for the ravens, which are intelligent and mischievous birds, and all have their own characters. One of the previous resident birds, their self-appointed leader, named Thor, would greet visitors with the words "Good Morning."

The scope of their intelligence is such that university students visit the Tower to study their behaviours and cognitive powers. They are believed to have an "understanding of past, present and future" (*historic-uk.com*) and to have intellectual abilities similar to those of chimpanzees or dolphins. Skaife explains that if humans had brains of the same size relative to that of their bodies, our heads would be twice as large as they are.

This intelligence makes them very curious by nature, sometimes naughty. They have been known to swoop and steal purses from visitors and hide the coins they find in them in various places in the Tower's grounds. The birds are the third most important reason for people visiting the Tower, with the Crown Jewels being the most popular attraction, followed by the Beefeaters. According to *historic-uk.com*, Skaife "shares his experiences with the ravens on social media, putting up pictures and videos almost daily".

Tower ravens tend to live longer than their wild counterparts with a good diet and veterinary care. Every week, with help from his three assistants, Skaife gives the birds a thorough health check. "Monitoring the birds' health is an important part of [the Ravenmaster's] job and he is in close contact with vets based at London Zoo, where he takes them when they fall ill", BBC News explains.

Every three weeks he trims the lifting feathers on their right wings to prevent them from flying too far afield. Despite having their wings trimmed, some ravens do go AWOL such as raven Grog who was last seen outside an East End pub and others have had to be sacked, like raven George who was dismissed for eating TV aerials. One of the birds, Muninn, was once lost for a week. Skaife got a call from a man in Greenwich, who thought a bird he had seen might be from the Tower. Skaife "talked him through catching her - a piece of chicken, a blanket and some gloves, and then he came and got her", as *historic-uk.com* describes it.

Skaife was introduced to the ravens by his predecessor Derek Coyle who became a Ravenmaster's assistant just two months after he joined the Yeoman Warders, aged 39. Coyle saw that Skaife had an affinity with the birds and that they got on well with him. Skaife trained with Coyle for five years as an assistant, before taking on the job himself when Coyle retired.

Although the tradition of employing a Ravenmaster only started relatively recently, the Tower of London dates from 1078 and the Yeomen Warders have been looking after it since 1485.

The job of Ravenmaster is difficult to get, even when you meet the essential requirements of the training and of being a Yeoman Warder. The pay is modest, but it is such an unusual occupation that only one person in the world can say it is their job.

The Sewer Hunters of Victorian London

FOR MOST PEOPLE, LIFE IN any industrialised city during the Victorian era was one of dire poverty. Wages were low, housing was pitiful and there was little in the way of healthcare provision. The vast majority lived in dreadful slums of which most of the elite class had no knowledge.

In 1851 Henry Mayhew published a four-volume work called *London Labour and the London Poor*, which has been described by the Smithsonian Institute as a piece of sociological journalism that documented the lives of working-class Londoners. He encountered those who recycled cigar ends and those who worked in other dismal and peculiar jobs such as the "toshers", who had arguably the worst job of all. These were men who went into the sewers looking for anything that might be of some value such as coins dropped in the street and swept into the gutters, cutlery and other metal items. They even collected bones and fragments of rope. They got this name because the items they retrieved from the sewers were known among these men as "tosh'. Although this occupation has long been obsolete in London, shockingly, it persists today in countries such as Bangladesh.

While the work itself was unpleasant, the financial rewards were high. According to Mayhew, on a good day, they made in excess of six shillings, more than £40 in today's terms, doing "the worst job ever", which meant walking for miles through the sewers. This made them among the best paid working-class earners in Victorian London. They saw themselves as above the mud-larks, who scavenged the Thames for coal, wood and rope, because their job was to seek out valuable items like gold and silver coins. As Mayhew puts it "they look down with a species of aristocratic contempt on the puny efforts of their less fortunate brethren the 'mud-larks' ".

Although self-employed, the toshers wore a uniform of canvas aprons and long coats with many capacious pockets. They also carried large bags on their backs in which to store the valuables they had collected. Each man was equipped with a lantern on his chest and all carried an 8 ft (2.5 metre) pole in the form of a hoe. These were used to search through excrement and to escape from quicksand-like pits full of detritus.

As the sewers became more dilapidated and increasingly dangerous, the thing that the sewer hunters feared most was still the rats. A single bite from a sewer rat could be fatal, and the rats would sometimes attack in hordes. One tosher told Mayhew "I often see as many as a hundred rats at once, and they're whoppers. . . they'd think nothing of tackling a man." He also claimed that the sewers were inhabited by wild hogs, saying that they had become "as ferocious as they are numerous". These were believed to inhabit the sewers in the Hampstead area of North London.

Another story perpetuated by the toshers but much more fervently believed was that of the "Queen Rat". According to historians Jacqueline Simpson and Jennifer Westwood: "This was a supernatural creature whose true appearance was that of a rat." She would make herself invisible in order to follow the toshers whilst they were at work. If she saw a man among them whom she fancied, she would transform her appearance into that of an attractive woman and accost him. If he gave her a good time, his luck was in and he would doubtless discover a large haul of valuables. As Mayhew puts it, "Although she did not look quite like a normal woman, with eyes that reflected light like an animal's and claws on her toes", the man was unlikely to notice this while he made love to her in the darkness. If she did lead him to become suspicious and he told anyone about his encounter with her, she would curse him with bad luck and he might drown or have some other sort of fatal accident.

Some of the other hazards the toshers encountered included being buried under a pile of rotten bricks. There was the possibility of drowning when the sluice gates were opened twice a day. Mayhew states: "If the sewer-hunter be not close to some branch sewer, so that he can run into it, whenever the opening of these sluice gates takes place, he must inevitably perish". These risks came alongside those of explosions due to the presence of sulfurated hydrogen. The "foul air" could also be instantly fatal if inhaled.

Mayhew describes the toshers generally as having a healthy complexion, which may have been because of the strength of their immune system due to the infectious conditions working in the sewers. As he puts it: "many of them know illness only by name". He states that the toshers put this down to what they believed were the health-giving qualities of the air they breathed in the sewers, so long as it was not the "foul air". He adds that "the sewer hunters, strange as it may appear, are certainly smart fellows, and take decided precedence of all the other 'finders' in London". Mayhew relates that they were known to the fraternity by nicknames such as Lanky Bill, Long Tom, One-eyed George and Short Armed Jack. Their real names were kept in secrecy.

In the 1840s entering the sewers without permission was legally banned because of the dangers this entailed. "They fears as how we'll get suffocated, but they don't care if we get starved" one tosher told Mayhew. The toshers reacted to this change in the law by changing their routine from entering the sewers at low tide to doing so under the cover of darkness. When they reached a grate, they were careful to cover their lanterns to avoid detection, which could mean a heavy fine or imprisonment. Ordinary citizens were likely to inform on them because of the large rewards that were offered.

According to the Smithsonian Institute, most toshers "worked in gangs of three or four men led by a veteran, who was frequently somewhere between 60 and 80 years old". These veterans knew where to find the items of value. They knew their way around thousands of miles of tunnels, many of which were less than 4 ft (1.2 metres) high. Nevertheless, they sometimes got lost in the maze-like sewer system if they strayed too far from the main branches, since the tunnels were not designed according to any recognisable pattern. This put them at risk of being in the sewer when the sluice gates were opened. Anyone who suffered from claustrophobia would be ill-suited to the job.

Historian Geri Watson, in her article "London Sewer Hunters", states that: "On good days when toshers were lucky, they found many articles such as plates, ladles, silver handled utensils, mugs and jewellery." The best of the finds were near the grates, with copper coins being particularly plentiful. It was not unusual to discover silver coins, such as sixpences and half crowns, while sometimes they were lucky enough to find gold half-sovereigns or even sovereigns. The profits were split among the gang members.

Although there is no evidence of sewer hunting before Mayhew reported it, it is likely to have been a long-standing tradition. A sewer system was introduced in London by the Romans and Henry VIII issued The Bill of Sewers in 1531. This led to the appointment of commissioners to oversee the maintenance of the tunnels in their own districts. The result was that there was no overall plan or map for the burgeoning sewer system.

By the time toshing was banned in the 1840s, due to safety concerns, London's sewers were in a very bad state of repair and the Thames, into which the effluent was discharged, was effectively dead. With 150 million tons being added year on year, the stench became intolerable in the summer months. In 1858 it was so bad that Parliament had to be evacuated. This was known as the "Great Stink".

Engineer Joseph Bazalgette was brought in to modernise the sewers. By 1866 most of Bazalgette's improved network was in place. Once this was done the toshers had to give up their lucrative trade, because of water from the Thames flowing into the sewers. The new sewers carried the waste to beyond the eastern edge of the city where it was processed in new treatment plants, thus putting an end to the stink. Bazalgette was knighted for his services to Londoners.

Professional Sleeping

SURPRISING AS IT MAY SEEM, some people are actually paid to go to sleep. This often occurs when companies encourage their employees to take an afternoon nap or siesta. More unusually it can also mean that people are paid to sleep for research purposes. Some can even be employed as bed testers.

In 2013 NASA recruited professional sleepers for 70 hours each at a rate of $18,000 at the Johnson Space Centre in Houston, Texas in order to help astronauts with difficulties they experience with sleeping in space. The participants were permitted "to chat with friends, study online courses and even to work remotely", but they were not allowed to leave their beds during the trial (*careeraddict.com*).

Other research opportunities are available, with hospitals and universities constantly seeking participants for their sleep research. These will usually measure brain waves, respiration, heart rhythm and muscle movement. Participants are sometimes healthy sleepers and sometimes those with sleep disorders, depending on the nature of the study. Those taking part need to be comfortable with being observed while they sleep as the researchers track their brains and their bodies.

Companies such as Facebook, Google and the Huffington Post encourage their employees to take an afternoon nap, even providing them with "energy pods" which are chairs specially designed to allow employees to recline and block out the sights and sounds of what is going on around them. Some even play calming music through built in speakers and include an alarm for "timed waking". The recommended time for napping is twenty minutes between the hours of 1pm – 4pm. Any later and it risks disrupting much needed night-time sleeping. Employees have said the nap makes them more able to meet the challenges of the rest of the working day, improving their productivity.

Some professional sleepers are employed as bed testers, testing mattresses and duvets for example. Some bed testers blog about their experience which helps manufacturers improve their products. Others are employed by hotel chains or bedding companies.

Although being paid to sleep may sound like a cushy job, for those who do it is demanding and painstaking. They have to work under pressure and often find themselves becoming perfectionists, even checking with a magnifying glass for hairs in the bathtub.

The web magazine *Hotel Chatter* profiled the role of Travelodge's Director of Sleep in 2006. He was paid to sleep on a selection of the hotel chain's 25,000 beds. He would also check how well sound-proofed the walls were and the suitability of the lighting in the room. Pillows, mattresses and duvets had to match up to his exacting standards to be suitable for a Travelodge bed.

The job, although highly sought after, is not as unusual as one might think. Jo Unsworth of London was employed by John Lewis department stores as a full-time duvet tester. She helped customers find their ideal bedding by sleeping in all the company's products. "Her personal favourite and recommendation is a big, thick, goose-down duvet", *payscale.com* has reported. Said Ms Unsworth: "My friends and family think I've got the best job in the world and they're probably right." (*careeraddict.com*). Her degree in Textile Management was crucial to her appointment.

For a temporary job bed testing, student Roisin Madigan was paid £1,000 to sleep in designer beds every day for a month. She worked for Simon Horn Ltd, a manufacturer of luxury beds which supplies them to the Savoy Hotel. She spent the daytime bed-testing, from 10am to 6pm, in various conditions imitating different traveller scenarios, with varying amounts of caffeine and alcohol first imbibed and different lighting, heat and sound conditions. As well as all these inconveniences, Madigan had the additional burden of having to sleep in the showroom while customers were passing by. She had to keep written records of her experiences and it was because of her writing skills that she was chosen out of hundreds of applicants.

In 2016, beds and bedding company Sealy Posturepedic set out to choose its very own "Sleep Ambassador". Seventy-year-old Lancashire pensioner Desmond Wilcox was selected from hundreds of applicants. Wilcox was well known by his friends and family for being able to fall asleep anywhere. His main hobbies in retirement are gardening and spending time in the "great outdoors". His job included testing the company's "beds, pillows and duvets as well as trialling a number of sleep experiences" (*Sealy Posturepedic*). These included testing sleep-aids and trying different diets and lifestyles to improve his sleep quality. Wilcox is now a member of the Deeper Sleeper Panel which consists of the five finalists for the job of Sleep Ambassador.

The first three full-time bed testers in China emerged in 2009. There are many more today. As one bed tester E. Zhuang told *Shanghai Daily*, "it is impossible to relax and enjoy the pleasure of hotel services if you must move from one hotel to another in different areas in a short time." Another, Candy Fu, said: "My work does not start when I stay at a hotel. I do a lot of research in advance." Bed tester Luca Wang said she has become much more meticulous since she started the job and has developed demanding and exacting standards. She even turns over the mattresses to ascertain the manufacturer's name.

Although the job may seem easy at first, with no educational requirements and work experience, in fact the bed tester must have the ability to submit quality reviews. The job requires making detailed observation of the hotel experience and to be able to see things from the point of view of different types of traveller, for example a business traveller or a mother and baby. According to Zhuang, "role playing is the difference between an ordinary customer and a professional hotel sleeper." This means she examines the hotel's various facilities including function rooms and gyms, as well as facilities in the local area, and issues such as time wasted in traffic in getting to and from the hotel.

Said Zhuang: "When [reviewing] my first Hyatt hotel everything was new and merited recording." But after visiting a few more Hyatts, finding distinctive features between the different hotels became more difficult and required closer observation.

Professional hotel sleeping in China started with the online travel agency Quanar.com and many travellers now base their decisions on where to stay on these reviews. Many five-star hotels now consider independent reviews to be an essential part of their marketing strategy. If issues are reported by the reviewer, the hotel will act to ensure this does not happen again.

Many hotel chains and websites are carrying out reviews of this kind which do not have the impartiality of an independent reviewer. Independent reviews are becoming increasingly sought after by hotels. "It's impossible to get a truly independent review from a hotel test sleeper hired by travel agency websites that co-operate with hotels for room booking and advertisement", Pu Jiayu, senior hotel editor at *Eastern Channel*, a travel magazine, told *Shanghai Daily*.

Swan Upping

SWANS MAY LOOK CALM, GLIDING effortlessly along the River Thames, but in fact their lives are fraught with danger. This could be from any one of a multiplicity of hazards facing them, which range from attacks by mink, dogs and foxes; fish-hooks; and hooligans with air rifles. Urban development on the riverside also restricts swans' nesting sites.

But the swan has a valuable ally in Her Majesty the Queen, among whose many titles is Seigneur of the Swans. By tradition she owns all mute swans on Britain's waterways, except those of which the monarchy has granted ownership to other parties. From the twelfth century a licensing system was established which granted ownership of swans to landed lords and institutions such as the universities, abbeys and livery companies. Those who were privileged enough to be granted ownership of swans would mark their beaks with their own insignia which were recorded on rolls of vellum, some of which still exist today. At present the ownership of swans is only granted to two livery companies and the Ilchester family, who own a few in Abbotsbury, Dorset.

In practice the Queen only exercises her rights over the swans on the River Thames. Once a year she sends out a party of envoys in rowing boats to count, measure and check the condition of them. Centuries ago, this was done on all of England's major rivers and tributaries.

Known as Swan Upping, the annual census, which still takes place on the Thames, takes five days and has been carried out in every year since the twelfth century. However, the purpose of the survey has changed since those days. In the middle ages swan was a delicacy served at banquets and feasts, but "today swan upping is all about conservation and education" (*Daily Mail*).

The party is led by the Queen's Swan Marker, a post currently held by David Barber, a seller of boat engines by trade, who has been leading these expeditions since 1993. Barber wears a traditional uniform of a scarlet jacket with gold braid, which he is careful to avoid soiling during the swan upping. "I've got enough gold braid that if I fell into the river, I'd drown" he mused in the *Washington Post*. He also wears a swan's feather in his cap.

He is accompanied by Her Majesty's Swan Warden who is a trained zoologist, and 20 liverymen from three livery companies. These are those of the Queen, the Vintners and the Dyers. The latter two are medieval London trade guilds which were granted ownership of some swans by the Crown in the fifteenth century. These livery men also wear traditional uniforms, "red for the Queen, white for the Worshipful Company of Vintners and blue for the Worshipful Company of Dyers", says the *Daily Mail*. Half the swans they capture are assigned to the Crown, and receive no tag, while the remaining number are divided up between the other two livery companies and tagged accordingly.

On the first day of the survey, a Monday in the third week of July, the swan uppers start their journey upstream from Abingdon to Sunbury-on-Thames, a distance of some 80 miles (130 km), in their wooden rowing skiffs. "It is called the Swan Upping, because we row *up* the river and pick *up* the swans" Barber explained. This stretch of the river is where the main concentration of breeding pairs is located. When the survey takes place, the cygnets are still being looked after by their parents.

When a group of cygnets is spotted, the oarsman shouts: "All up" and the boats rapidly encircle the brood. They are then grabbed by the necks and torsos and hauled aboard. Their legs are tied behind their backs and they are then quickly weighed, measured, given a health check and tagged before being returned to the water. The parent swans, the male known as a cob and the female known as a pen, look understandably irate. Adult swans are well known to be belligerent, especially in defence of their young. One of the uppers reported in 2018 that an adult swan had gnashed him with its claws, which protrude from its webbed feet. "You might think it'd be the powerful wings or the honking great beak, but no" he told the *Washington Post.* "They eat grass. There's nothing to the beak" he explained. "They might nibble you a bit, but that's it." These adult swans will have been counted in past censuses, so it is only the still flightless cygnets that the uppers are concerned with.

Zoologist Chris Perrins, an Oxford University professor, who at the time of writing holds the title of Swan Warden, has participated in the swan survey every year since the 1970s "when the swan population went into sudden decline", according to the *Daily Mail.* Perrins and his colleagues found that many swans had swallowed poisonous lead fishing weights. Once these weights were banned in the 1980s, the swan population swiftly grew back to a healthy level. "The population had about doubled then, nationally" said Perrins in the *Daily Mail* in 2014. "There are about 1,000 swans along this stretch of the river, still less than the 1950s level."

During Barber's tenure as Swan Marker, numbers have fluctuated wildly. "The numbers are a concern" he is reported as saying in the *Telegraph online.* "It proves why we need this tradition more than ever" he added. "We found a lot of cygnets in ones and twos, which suggests mink could have been around, snatching them. They're becoming a real problem" he said in 2016. In February 2018 the Department for Food and Rural Affairs (Defra) reported that dozens of swans had died of avian flu. Nonetheless, in July 2018 they counted 32 cygnets in eight broods by the time they had reached Eton College. Barber said this was not bad at all. Swans sometimes become entangled in plastic rubbish or fishing lines which can be quickly removed by the uppers.

As the *Daily Mail* puts it: "Most of the swan-uppers are full-time watermen who work on commuter vessels, party boats and tugs". They see swan upping as a working holiday that allows them to indulge in an old tradition. One of the rituals of the flotilla is that when they reach Windsor Castle, they lay down their oars and to stand and raise a toast to "The Queen -- Seigneur of the Swans". The traditional end to the survey is a pub lunch.

On the 20 July 2009 the Queen attended the Swan Upping ceremony. This was the first visit by the monarch in centuries. The ceremony has only been cancelled on one occasion in 900 years. This was in 2012 when bad weather forced its abandonment between Sunbury and Windsor.

The former Liberal Democrat MP Norman Baker has described swan upping as a relic of the feudal times. He explained his views in the *Guardian*: "Swan upping is harmless in itself, but it masks a wider anachronism which is unhealthy and unfair". What he may not have realised was that the two posts of Swan Marker and Swan Warden only date back to 1993 when the thirteenth century job of "Master of the Swans" was divided between them.

It is not known which monarch was the first "Seigneur of the Swans", but Stephen Freeth of the Vintners' Company explains to me that the rights of the Vintners and the Dyers probably date back to at least Edward IV (1461-83).

Contrasting with Baker, retired houseboat owner Richard Poad told the *Washington Post*: "The tradition is wonderful and it's important to educate the young". He said the uppers of today carried out their duties with great professionalism, while in the past it been a bit of a "pub crawl".

I am told by Stephen Freeth that until a few years ago they monitored the health of the swans all year round, but this is now the responsibility of several charities which the company sponsors. Principally these are Swan Lifeline and the Swan Sanctuary. They are in contact with traffic police and other organisations which they often call upon to give assistance. He says that the company supported the ban on lead weights in fishing tackle in the 1980s, which has led to the great rise in swan numbers.

An expert on swans from earlier times was Norman Ticehurst, who commented in 1926 that the royal licence for ownership of the swans accompanied by the age-old tradition of Swan Upping had probably saved the birds from extinction. Perrins agrees. Aristocrats sought the status that a pair of swans residing in their moat or lake would bring them. "It is rare to preserve such a big, edible, easily caught bird in a heavily populated area", he stated. "If it weren't for the snob appeal of owning swans, we probably wouldn't have them."

Tea Tasting

THE PROCESS OF TEA TASTING is also known as degustation. The job of tea taster requires gifted professionals and can be seen as an art which also requires scientific skills. Tea tasters need to be able to "understand and differentiate the contents of taste-giving alkaloids in tea samples", according to *streetdirectory.com*. They must also be able to identify fragrances released by the samples. Knowledge of tea plantations and how they work is also essential.

To embark on a career as a tea taster, one should know about the cultivation and manufacturing processes involved in the tea industry. The tea taster should know about different grades and varieties of tea as well as what will be the characteristics of the resulting beverage. A good tea taster must not only abstain from smoking, but also avoid alcohol and strongly spicy foods.

A degree in Agriculture, Food Science or Horticulture is a good starting point for a career in the tea industry. A good taster can make as much money as a software engineer, but the job involves outdoor work on the tea plantation as well as attending tea auctions and carrying out tastings, which will appeal to some people.

Tea drinking has a long history and the drink is ever popular which means there is always a place for tea tasting and the tea industry. Tea tasters should provide themselves with a good book on scientific tea testing, tasting and blending techniques. They will develop their skills over time as they learn from experience.

Popular brands of tea need to ensure consistency in the flavour of their products. This is important for tea traders when they make purchasing decisions. They can only purchase large quantities of tea if they are sure it will provide this. The taste of tea varies from plucking to plucking, so attaining this consistency involves the blending of different types of tea. This is where tea tasters come in. They are the only people who are knowledgeable enough about teas to define the nuances of its taste.

Prices vary from one crop to another. In countries which grow tea on a large scale, auctions are commonplace. Each plantation sends its product to a stock exchange centre such as the ones in Colombo and Kolkata where auctions take place every week. Before a sale, the tea taster must be satisfied with the quality and price. To assess these, tea tasters everywhere use the same method. They all use the same equipment, the same amount of tea and boiling water as well as a standard brewing time of five minutes.

There are three stages involved in tea tasting. The first is to assess the dry leaf, the second to test the infusion and the final stage is the tea tasting itself.

When assessing the leaf, the taster looks to see if it corresponds to the right leaf grade. Colour and optics are also assessed. The leaf is checked for cleanliness. This involves looking for any signs of dust or stems from the tea plant. The taster must next smell the infused tea leaf to discern its aroma.

The final and most important step is the actual tea testing which is a similar process to wine tasting. The tea taster either uses a spoon or sips directly from the cup. With this sip of tea, the taster should be able to ascertain its character and strength as well as its aroma.

The tea taster sucks the tea sample whilst making a slurping sound caused by the tea hitting the taste buds at high speeds so that the taster can evaluate the quality of what he or she is tasting. After each tasting, the liquid is generally spat back into a spittoon and the verdict is cast before the taster moves on to the next example.

The flavour of tea and characteristics of leaves including colour, size and shape are graded using the specialist language of the tea industry, designed to describe the overall quality of the beverage. Once the tea has been tested it is graded and a value placed on it based on market trends, availability and demand.

It takes about five years training to develop the skills of a professional tea taster. By this time the taster must know the entire range of tea varieties and be able to carry out a blind tasting. This requires the tea taster to be able to identify not only the country of origin but the region within that country as well. The Tetley Tea Academy explains to me that trainees will "learn their tasting language, spend time in different tea gardens around the world, [learn about] the crops and drying processes and taste almost 100,000 different teas." There is no formal examination for becoming a Master Blender with Tetley or any other company that they know of.

One professional tea taster is known to have insured his taste buds for £1,000,000 after years of training enabled him to become a master blender. This is Sebastian Michaelis, who claims to be able to taste and grade any of the world's 1,500 tea varieties in just 15 seconds. He is a philosophy graduate who changed direction to a graduate training programme to become a tea taster.

At the time of writing Michaelis works for Tetley where he uses the "slurp and spit" procedure to judge what he described as the "zing, colour, sparkle and body" of a cup of tea, admitting to *Sky News* that "the beverage now dominates his life". He added that in pursuit of this career he has travelled round the world visiting tea producers and has had to "understand everything about tea".

Tetley says its experts can taste as many as 1,000 different teas in a day as they strive to keep a consistent blend for their popular brand. Michaelis explains that weather conditions affecting tea plantations, such as the amount of sunshine and rain they get, will significantly affect the taste of the tea. This is similar to the effect of the weather on the wine industry.

Giles Oakley, a Tetley's Tea master blender, told the *Guardian* that he was one of the lucky few from hundreds of applicants who put in for the position. He underwent a day of tests which included one for colour blindness since a tea taster needs to "be able to distinguish the differing colours as well as the flavours of the leaves", as the *Guardian* put it.

New recruits earn a modest salary and will spend their first few months getting to know hundreds of types of tea, sipping them one by one, memorising their names and distinguishing features as well as picking up the various forms of specialist language used by different companies in the tea industry. The actual tea tasting is only one small part of the job. Tasters need to be able to understand the whole process of the tea industry from crop planting to supermarket shelves, said Oakley.

After a thorough education in blending to satisfy consumer demand for consistency of flavour, a lengthy training trip to tea-growing countries is undertaken. This involves learning about the production process, the trading of tea and getting to know networks of tea traders with whom they will be doing business.

"The first experience of a tea auction is terrifying because you are spending vast sums of money with the nod of your head", according to Oakley. He described having a "passion" for a drink that is usually taken for granted.

Put simply, tea tasting is all about being able to ascertain the nuances of tea and its flavours and aromas. This takes many years of practice. If one assumes a taster tested about 500 cups per day over 5 years, it becomes clear how much experience they would have gained, and how much time they would have spent on tea tasting.

Town Criers

WHEN MOST OF THE POPULATION could not read or write, one of the few ways that news could be spread to the population was by the Town Crier. This would include royal proclamations, market day announcements, bylaws and advertisements. David Mitchell, author of *For Crying Out Loud, The Story of the Town Crier and the Bellman, Past and Present*, describes them as "walking, talking newspapers and pioneer outside broadcasters". From the eighteenth century the uniform for these people was a red robe with gold braid, white breeches, black boots and a distinctive three-cornered hat. The town crier's uniform was similar to that worn by the Mayor and usually incorporated the colours of the crier's town.

They would draw the public's attention by ringing a handbell and call out their announcements in a loud voice. Historically, if the announcement was very important, the crier would follow the exact wording set out by the relevant authority, usually the Sheriff or the City Assembly. But for proclamations of a more mundane nature such as market day announcements or local bylaws, the crier would adopt his own personal style, for example idiosyncratic ways of speaking or putting his announcements into rhyme, a practice emulated by some modern-day town criers.

Surprisingly, many women were employed as town criers as well as men. Sometimes the job was carried out by a husband and wife team, where the husband often made the proclamation and the wife rang the handbell. David Mitchell was appointed Town Crier of Chester in 1997 and joined by his wife Julie in the role in 1998.

Town criers operated in other countries too, such as the Netherlands where a gong was used instead of a handbell. As the British Empire extended across the world, the role of town crier spread with it. There are currently town criers' guilds in Canada, the USA and Australia, continuing the tradition. Town criers are represented in England by the Ancient and Honourable Guild of Town Criers and the Loyal Company of Town Criers.

Town criers still attract the public's attention by ringing a handbell and calling out "oyez, oyez, oyez" before making their announcements. "Oyez" is a Norman French word meaning "listen". From 1066, this call has been heard in England, but David Mitchell disputes the claim that the role of town crier was introduced by William the Conqueror -- wrongly deduced, he says, from the Bayeux Tapestry. This does feature two bellmen, but in a scene which depicts England before the invasion, at the funeral of Edward the Confessor.

In fact, town criers arrived many centuries earlier in other cultures. In ancient Rome a crier known as the "praeco" would summon free citizens to the "ekklesia", a meeting where voting took place. Similar meetings occurred in ancient Greece, from where the term "ekklesia" is derived, but voters were summoned by a police force of slaves brandishing ropes.

Little is known about the proclaimers of ancient Egypt, but a tomb dated 2230 BC. depicts a scribe making announcements from a scroll that he has probably written himself. In the Book of Proverbs in the Bible, completed in about 700 BC, announcements are made to the people in public places. Interestingly, the crier is described as a woman.

According to David Mitchell, in pre-industrial Britain, town criers would have been as familiar as buskers, Big Issue sellers, obituaries and lost and found notices. In fact, the word to "publish" originally meant to proclaim aloud rather than to make public by printing. Sometimes the crier was engaged by a male member of the public to have his wife "cried down" or "decried by the bellman" if he considered her to be too headstrong.

Criers were protected by law and any act against them was considered treasonable. This was necessary because some of their proclamations were unpopular, such as news of tax increases. Hence came the phrase "don't shoot the messenger" which is still used today. It was also important before the days of modern communication "to make provision in your will for the bellman to announce the news of your passing to friends and relatives", according to David Mitchell.

Before the invention of printing a crier would, after making an announcement, nail the paper on which it was written to a post, so that the literate minority could get informed. This is the origin of the term "posting a notice". Also, newspapers such as the *Liverpool Daily Post*, the *Lancashire Post* and the *Yorkshire Post* take their names from these origins. With the invention of the telegraph, followed by that of the telephone and the radio, the formerly essential town crier was nearly consigned to history, only to be rediscovered in the latter part of the twentieth century.

There are few records of what was proclaimed, but along with their male counterparts, female criers feature on the historical record. The best known of these is Betty Dick of Dalkeith, Scotland. She used a large wooden trencher which she hit with a spoon. She was succeeded by Peggy Haswell, who preferred to use a hand bell. After her came Jessie Gervald, followed by Grizzie Brown, known as "Bell Greasy". After she left the job, the magistrates decided a drum would be better than a handbell and the Bell Wives gave way to the Town Drummer, whose services were much more expensive.

When war broke out in 1914 Albert Blaker, Chertsey Town Crier, became enlisted and his wife Mary Ann took over his duties as a "temporary' measure". When he returned from the war, his wife refused to relinquish the job. Local press described her incorrectly as "England's first woman town crier". She held the office for 26 years before she passed away.

The historical record of the names of town criers in Chester where David Mitchell is currently employed is patchy and incomplete. The same is true for towns up and down the country. The status of their roles was not sufficient for them to be recorded for posterity. Unlike the record of the 629 mayors who have ever held office in Chester, David Mitchell explains, "we only know the names of only 30 of Chester's historic criers and bellmen".

It is only when we come to John Jeffrey, who was Chester's town crier from 1874-1897, that the records are sufficient to shed a good deal of light on the crier. These include photographic evidence and his notebook which records his proclamations in an attractive copperplate hand. His previous employment included a wide variety of jobs including collector of market rents, chapel keeper and railway inspector.

After his death in 1903 Jeffrey was described as the city's last bellman. No one could have predicted the revival of his trade in the second half of the twentieth century. In 1978 the post of Town Crier was re-instated in Chester, with the appointment of Tom Clarkson.

Many local authorities in England and Wales revived the office of Town Crier during the late twentieth century. These were generally honorary or part-time posts. According to the *Shropshire Star*, in 2020 there were well over 200 British criers. They are mainly active on ceremonial occasions, at civic functions and charity events.

Peter Moore (1939-2009) was Town Crier for the Cities of London and Westminster along with serving a few Greater London boroughs, the Mayor of London and the London Tourist Board. Moore held the post of Town Crier of London for 31 years. He was a frequent visitor on his official business to London landmarks including the Tower of London and Piccadilly Circus. When Peter Moore died in December 2009, his funeral was attended by fellow town criers from across the country.

According to the Corporation of London, Alan Myatt is employed by them as the Common Cryer of the City of London on an ad-hoc basis. He is also the town crier for Covent Garden and other assorted settings in London. Myatt is also, at the time of writing, employed by the City of Gloucester, as well as a few other towns in England.

Many bygone trades have been consigned to history, for example the Dog Whipper and the Night Soil Man. However, the office of town crier is one that catches the public's attention, so despite the revolution in information technology the job has been revived in many towns and cities as a tourist attraction and to improve the public image of the local authorities.

Umbrella Making

THE ORIGINAL PALM-LEAFED UMBRELLA WAS a status symbol, but since their invention, over 3,500 years ago, umbrellas became increasingly sophisticated. Over time, as new materials were developed, their durability improved, while more complex mechanisms for opening and closing the canopy made them easier to use.

Palm-leafed parasols first emerged in ancient Egypt, used by the nobility and royalty to ensure that their skin was fashionably pale. Because of the lack of rain in the desert environment they did not see the need to develop umbrellas to protect against rain. The first rain protection umbrellas appeared in China in the eleventh century BC, usually made using leather. Prohibitively expensive to buy, they were used only by the ruling elite. The highest-ranking citizens had multi-tiered umbrellas. They carried over to ancient Greece and Rome, during the first century AD, and "it was recorded that both Greek and Roman women had umbrellas that could open and close" (*umbrellahistory.com*). These were often carried by slaves on their behalf. They were used only by women, before falling out of use in the dark ages.

Umbrellas did not return to Europe until the early part of the Renaissance and became popular there in the seventeenth century, or the sixteenth by some accounts. They were even used in religious ceremonies by the Roman Catholic and Orthodox churches. By the start of the eighteenth century, more waterproof materials started to be used and a new design of umbrella was introduced that was both lightweight and chic. It was not long before a "parapluie" became a must-have accessory for every Parisian lady.

Early umbrellas provided less protection from the rain than today's examples. However, the basic canopy structure remains largely unchanged. In Europe they were seen as a feminine article which men preferred to do without.

It was not until the mid-eighteenth century that European men started to take up the use of umbrellas. The Englishman, Jonas Hanway, a well-known eccentric and philanthropist, challenged the social etiquette that umbrellas were for female use alone. He started to carry a sturdier, more male-oriented one in public. It took three decades of his stubbornness before the idea of men carrying umbrellas caught on first in England and soon after in Europe generally. According to *kaufmannmercantile.com*: "The Duke of Wellington, victor at Waterloo, was said to have one weighing 4.5 kg (10 lb) with a concealed dagger in its handle."

Modern umbrellas are lighter and more durable and better at protecting the user from the elements, be these rain, snow, wind or sun. The umbrella has evolved into an up to date device produced by the modern umbrella manufacturing industry, although still generally assembled by hand from the various parts.

The materials used for the canopy have changed considerably since the first umbrellas appeared. In the ancient world taffeta, silk, cotton, leather and linen were popular. These were later replaced by a weave of silk and wool or silk and cotton and more recently nylon and acetate. Modern umbrella canopies are generally made from microfibre fabrics (nylon taffeta) that are coated with water repellent finishes. The cloth must be cut into several (usually eight) pieces before the canopy is assembled because the mechanism for opening and closing it does not allow for the use of a single piece of cloth.

In 1928 Hans Haupt invented the pocket umbrella, but it was not until 1969 that Bradford E. Phillips invented the modern closing mechanism. In modern umbrellas, steel replaces whalebone ribs and stretchers. The development of steel was a boon but designs using fibreglass and carbon fibre continue to be experimented with.

New designs continue to abound, with many new patents being registered every year. This includes experimental umbrellas that can withstand winds of up to 62 miles (100 km) per hour and be turned inside out without being wrecked. At the time of writing most modern umbrellas are manufactured in China where there are thousands of companies building them. Although new designs have made them more lightweight, many of them are of poor quality and everyone is familiar with the sight of broken umbrellas in the gutters after a big storm. The higher quality ones are worth the extra expense and will last much longer.

Quality umbrellas are still manufactured by a few companies in London. James Ince & Sons is Britain's oldest, "founded in Spitalfields in 1805, and now operating in a modest factory next to the canal in Vyner Street", as *spitalfieldslife.com* describes it.

Fifth generation umbrella maker Terry Coleman was the longest serving member of the trade still working in the East End, when he was interviewed in 2011. He told *Spitalfields Life*: "We are all umbrella makers in my family, my father, his father and his father, all of my aunts and uncles were umbrella makers," He added: "I've been an umbrella maker from when I left school at the age of 14 -- there was no choice!" He went on to say that he actually started working for his father's umbrella manufacturing business in his spare time while he was still at school.

When interviewed, Coleman worked for Richard Ince, of James Ince & Son, who has the proud distinction of being the person who built Mary Poppins's umbrella for the Disney movie. Before this he worked for Ince's father, James. Both Coleman and Ince come from families with a long history of umbrella making and noticed the marked drop in sales at the end of the last century, as cheaper umbrellas from countries such as China took over the market.

James Ince & Sons Ltd was once a major manufacturer in the City of London with a prime location in Bishopsgate and a large number of workers. When the government ruled, during the 1980s, that umbrella makers should be treated as employees rather than as self-employed as they had been for generations, this hit the profitability of the business, which was already suffering from the influx of cheap imports.

Coleman described how he used to operate a small workshop of his own in Hackney which made umbrellas for the Inces. These ranged from a 16 inch (40.6 cm) size right up to a 10 foot (3 metre) diameter. "I would say we had the monopoly on golfing umbrellas" he said. "Golf was still a top-end pursuit in the 1960s, so the market accommodated an expensive umbrella." He added: "One day in 1963 I went in and there was a bundle of golf umbrellas on imported metal frames and Richard's grandfather said: 'I don't know if this is going to catch on' – but now that's all there is."

London's umbrella manufacturing business started in Spitalfields two centuries ago. The predecessors of the current makers built articles that were made from whalebone and silk which was woven locally. They were part of a plethora of skilled artisans working in the East End. "It's nice to make something" Coleman mused as he looked admiringly at the bundle of hand-made wooden shafts that represented his day's work. From the eighteenth century onwards, generations of London's umbrella makers have passed on the "knowledge, techniques and language" which are known only to them. (*Spitalfields Life*).

Historically, umbrellas have gone from being an item used by the aristocratic elite to an essential used by the general public. For several millennia, the rudimentary design of umbrellas has remained pretty much unchanged. Meanwhile, the materials used to construct them have developed from the earliest palm leaved umbrellas of ancient Egypt to modern, artificial materials, along with the latest opening and closing devices.

Verderers

THE OFFICE OF VERDERER WAS introduced after the Norman Conquest to look after the 60 royal hunting grounds and the animals that inhabited them, in particular wild boar and deer. Verderers were responsible for upholding forest law and for investigating and reporting minor offences such as poaching and the illegal felling of timber. They also dealt with the encroachment of illegal enclosures and buildings.

The royal hunting grounds were established by William the Conqueror and the word verderer is derived from the Norman French word "vert" meaning "green" and referring to woodland. Verderers are still responsible today for the Forest of Dean, the New Forest and Epping Forest, formerly known as Waltham Forest.

The earliest reference to a verderer in England dates from 1216, whereas the names of verderers are recorded for the first time in 1221. There were usually four verderers for every royal forest, each responsible for a different area of it.

By the fifteenth and sixteenth centuries forest law was in decline and verderers began to lose control of the forests, with poaching endemic and elections of verderers becoming increasingly infrequent. The forests began to disintegrate as the main duties of the verderers became limited to the gift and sale of trees.

The state of the forests and that of the office of verderer improved under Queen Elizabeth I when legislation was introduced to protect timber for the construction of warships. This meant that the verderers were much better organised in the distribution of fuel wood to the inhabitants of the forest.

In the early seventeenth century there was a marked increase in the use of charcoal in the iron industry, which led to widespread deforestation. This meant that the role of the verderers became increasingly relevant once again. In 1668 the Dean Forest (Reforestation) Act made provision to create enclosures to produce timber.

By 1788, with the monarchy no longer interested in hunting deer, a government commission found the appointment of verderers and other ancient forest offices was little more than ceremonial. They were usually bestowed as a favour on influential gentlemen residing in the locality. The conviction and punishment of poachers and others was by now mainly in the jurisdiction of the magistrates' court, not the verderers' court. Before the magistrates took over most of their law enforcement duties, the verderers had the power to impose sentences of death or transportation.

In 1838, however, verderers were given new powers to enforce the Enclosures Act, resulting in hundreds of convictions for encroachments such as putting up buildings and quarrying.

The protection of the venison continued to be an official role of the verderers, even after 1855, when the deer had been removed from the forests, because of rampant poaching. But the deer did return to many royal forests in the 1940s and protecting them is still one of the verderers' main duties.

In 1927 the Forestry Act set up the Forestry Commission which is now responsible for upholding forest byelaws. This meant that the role of verderers changed to that of conservators and the role of the verderers' court was further curtailed.

Forest of Dean Verderers date from at least 1218. As the last vestige of feudal forest governance, there are currently four of them in a tradition dating back 800 years. They are elected by the "freeholders of Gloucestershire at the Gloucester Court", itself an ancient tradition, now carried out by council officials. The verderers serve for life or until they are no longer able to carry out their duties. To become one of their number you must be of good character and reside within the forest parishes. They are not paid, but by tradition are "entitled to a doe and a buck a year from the forest, a bundle of wood and a bag of coal" (*verderers.co.uk*). However, nobody has exercised these rights in recent history.

Today they work closely with the Forestry Commission and local authorities, commenting on local planning applications. They also liaise with these organisations concerning diseases that affect trees such as ash, larch, oak and chestnut and manage the wild boar population of the forest. In general, their duties pertain to anything that could be detrimental to the forest. The verderers meet quarterly in their courthouse, known as the Speech House, located in the forest. This was originally built to serve as a hunting lodge for Charles II in 1669.

There are two other verderers' courts in the UK, one at Lyndhurst in the New Forest, and one at Epping that serves the royal forest there.

The New Forest was established by William the Conqueror as a hunting ground in the eleventh century. Today there are ten verderers of the New Forest who, similarly to the Forest of Dean verderers, work with the Forestry Commission, the National Trust, Natural England and local authorities, commenting on planning applications within the forest, such as those for roads, new car parks and camping sites to recreational facilities.

The duties of the verderers of the New Forest are primarily concerned with upholding the rights and responsibilities of the commoners, that is, those who exercise the right of the public to graze livestock on common land. They had been responsible for collecting commoners' Crown rents, but this became uneconomic over time. Nonetheless the verderers continue to assert this right symbolically "by firing a ritual shot over the land once a year", according to Sarah Nield in *Forest Law and the Verderers of the New Forest*.

They aim to preserve the traditional character and beauty of the forest. Together they constitute the Court of Verderers, also known as the Swaimote. This still has some powers and has a duty to deal with misdemeanours such as illegal enclosures and a range of other issues.

Early records of the verderers appointed to the Royal Forest of Epping, since the thirteenth century, are patchy. At this time the forest covered much of Essex. By the mid-eighteenth century the size of the forest was down to

3,500 acres (1,416 hectares) but today it stands at more than 6,000 acres (2,428 hectares).

The current duties and responsibilities of the office were set out in the Epping Forest Act of 1878. This act confirmed their office but took away their legal powers and instead made them responsible for the conservation of the forest. Today the verderers are elected every seven years by the commoners of the forest, two for the northern parishes, and two for the southern ones. In order to be appointed to this role, they must be inhabitants of the forest, just as they are in the Forest of Dean and the New Forest. They must have a comprehensive knowledge of the forest and the communities around it as well as of matters relating to forest management. They are the unpaid, voluntary, representatives of the commoners of the forest. It is their duty to uphold their rights of the commoners and make sure they carry out their obligations. They are also members of the Epping Forest Committee of the City of London and report to the Superintendent of the forest and other officials.

The office of verderer is an ancient one, originally designed for law enforcement, but which over time became more ceremonial. Today verderers have important responsibilities protecting the forests, working alongside organisations dedicated to heritage and conservation in Britain.

Voice-Over Artists

VOICE-OVER IS AN OFF-CAMERA dialogue or commentary where the individual speaking is not seen in the production. These scripts are played "over" or during a visual media production or a radio broadcast.

This often occurs during advertisements on TV. It can also be used to embellish the plot or storyline of a broadcast drama, documentary, movie, sports programme or other television show. Radio advertisements also use voice-over artists but, usually speaking in a different manner such as a slightly "over the top" style. Radio presenters and DJs are also considered to be voice-over artists.

Although there are now hundreds of TV channels and online outlets which have increased the scope of the voice-over industry, the competition is still extremely fierce, due in part to the availability of voice-over casting websites and electronic self-submissions. The best evidence of suitability as a commercial voice-over artist is previous experience. Another factor in the competition for this work is that celebrities are increasingly used to voice commercials.

Sometimes voice actors are used to provide voices for animated characters. With this type of voice-over there is more freedom in voicing as there is no need to match a dubbed actor. On some occasions this is done by famous actors. To name just a few: Angelina Jolie has voiced several cartoon characters including Master Tigress in Kung Fu Panda, Lola in Shark Tale and Grendel's mother in Beowulf. Cameron Diaz voiced Princess Fiona in the Shrek films and Brad Pitt can be heard in a number of roles such as that of Patch in King of the Hill and Sinbad in Sinbad: Legend of the Seven Seas.

Narration is used to provide a running commentary and to convey information to the audience. This is used in both drama and documentaries. The voice actor must enact the script allocated to the narrator.

Dub vocalisation is the dubbing of the voices of actors speaking in a foreign language in a film or television series. Unlike this practice, voice-over translation is a technique where the original soundtrack can still be heard in the background. This method is usually used in news reports and other documentaries to translate the words of interviewees who are speaking in a foreign language. Sometimes translation voice-overs are used to replace the original soundtrack, for example in movies that are sold abroad.

Automated dialogue replacement (ADR) is where the original lines spoken by the actors are rerecorded by them at a later date. This sometimes called "looping". It can be used to change lines or improve pronunciation. In the UK this process is known as "post-synchronisation" or simply "post-sync".

Automated announcements, in their simplest form, are pre-recorded messages like the well-known warning to "mind the gap" on the London Underground introduced in 1969. An example of a much more complicated system is the speaking clock, where the full message is put together from fragments such as "eighteen" and "minutes past". To give another example, the word "twelve" is used for both "twelve o'clock" and "six, twelve". These automated messages are also used on buses, trains and on-hold messages on the phone. With current technology it would be possible to use computer-generated voices for all these services, but it is generally assumed that the public would rather hear a human voice.

"Although it may seem like an easy job it does require hard work, talent and dedication", according to *thecareerproject.com.* A good clear voice is a prerequisite but the job also requires the abilities to "read and speak well" with "the right attitude and tone" (*thecareerproject.com).* A voice artist should be able to convey a real sense of emotion in order to make what they are saying believable. Depending on the content of the production, a voice artist will be asked to speak in a number of different ways. For example, for an advertisement, the speaker will probably be required to convey a sense of excitement or cheerfulness while for a public information broadcast, they must put it across with a sense of urgency

Even an experienced voice artist may be required to read a script several times before the client is satisfied. This may be because the script can be read in several different ways, with different emphases and pauses, each conveying a different message. For this job, one's voice must be one's best asset.

Although the job is not easy, "getting voice-over jobs is a little more difficult than actually doing them", as *thecareerproject.com* puts it. There is a lot of competition and clients usually use a few, talented voice artists with a good track record. Experienced voice artists earn ten times as much as those at entry level as their experience is much in demand. Amongst top ranking artists are celebrities such as James Corden, Dame Helen Mirren, the late Sir Sean Connery and Sir Ranulph Fiennes.

Anyone wanting to make their way into voice-over must in the first instance have a demo CD made. It is better to do this in a recording studio with professional assistance. Agents can be useful in helping someone make their CD demo and can also help them find auditions and gigs.

Some recording studios allow aspiring voice artists to record their voices of which they will keep a record on file, in case the speaker is suitable for one of their projects. But, as Carol Hanzel of Carol Hanzel Casting New York put it to the entertainment industry magazine *Backstage*: "While anyone can submit himself or herself online, we only work with established agents." This is also true of many other casting businesses.

Being in possession of a good voice, but not having the skills and training, is of no use in this business. Many established voice actors recommend taking elocution (voice) lessons. Sometimes an acting degree and experience in this field is useful, since the voice-over job is basically that of an actor. "You have to know how to articulate and where to emphasise punctuation, and acting has helped with that", voice-over artist Eric Nelson told *Backstage*. Canadian voice-artist Mandy Steckelberg, who has worked widely in the USA, told the magazine that the job is suitable for a "straightforward, compassionate, intelligent story-teller".

"A good voice talent has an internal clock", explained another voice-over expert, David de Vries. "So, when the casting director says, 'I need this copy read in 28.7 seconds' you'll land it". According to de Vries this is a natural ability that cannot be taught, which means that voice over is not for everyone.

According to *Backstage*, the most important attributes for voice-over are "believability and communication ability". Enjoying the work is also necessary. As the former singer Sara Krieger told the publication: "I got into voiceovers to make a living supporting my music. I fell in love with voiceover and never went back to the music".

Other necessary skills include being able to put a message across, convey an emotion, and to "nail it first time", said Krieger. She explained that the job used to be about vocal type, but now it is more about how one reads a script. One must often sound conversational, as if talking to a friend or "selling something without sounding like you're selling something". Some casting companies spend more time auditioning their voice-over actors than they do with their on-camera characters.

Krieger has also worked as a voice coach for would-be voice-over artists. When seeking this work, it is best to take classes or participate in workshops with professionals before creating a demo. It is necessary to prepare for this by finding one's best range and styles before deciding what roles to work in. "You need to identify where you fit as opposed to thinking you can do anything", said Krieger.

British voice artist Joanna Ruiz explained in the *Guardian* that adult female artists are often called upon to voice the words of small boys because their voices are lighter and, in any case, employing children involves too much red tape. She got into the business while studying at the Royal Welsh College of Music and Drama. She sang in a band there and was introduced to a woman who sang advertising jingles who suggested she did the same. Someone at the recording studios encouraged her to apply for a part in a re-recording of Caspar the Friendly Ghost. She practised hard and landed the lead part in this cartoon drama.

Ruiz describes how cartoons are easier to voice than advertisements where artists must sound enthusiastic about products they may not really be interested in. “The trick is to smile while you’re talking because that makes your voice sound bright and cheery”, she said. For Ruiz working on an animated production is like a holiday. “You’re there with all the other actors and the interaction makes the script come alive.”

Volcanology

"A VOLCANOLOGIST IS A HIGHLY qualified specialist in geophysics who studies both active and inactive volcanoes" (*careerexplorer.com*). The active ones are studied in order to try to understand the movement and formation of molten rock, also known as magma, under the Earth's surface. Inactive volcanoes are useful sources of information for volcanologists too where they study rock formations resulting from eruptions sometimes as long as tens of thousands of years ago. The overall aim of volcanologists is to try to understand how and why volcanic activity takes place, when volcanoes are likely to erupt and their effect on humans and their environment, as well as how they have affected the history of the Earth.

The word volcanology is derived from the name of the Roman god of fire, Vulcan. This field of study has a long history. The Greeks and Romans believed volcanic activity was the responsibility of the god of fire. The eruption of Mount Vesuvius in 79 AD which destroyed the Roman city of Pompeii gave it the reputation as "one of the most destructive volcanoes in history", according to *sciencing.com*. A detailed account of what happened was made by Pliny the Elder, who witnessed it but died while investigating it, and his nephew Pliny the Younger. This marked the start of the study of volcanic activity.

A text by the German Friedrich Wilhelm Heinrich Alexander von Humboldt was published in 1808, called *Voyage de Humboldt et Bonpland*. He scientifically described his findings in the aftermath of the eruption of Mount Chimborazo in Ecuador. One very large eruption, that of Mount

Tambora in Indonesia in 1815, was seen as significant enough to merit a study a century later, when scientists eventually tried to piece together what happened. This was so large that it blocked out the sun in much of the northern hemisphere for several months, leaving a year without summer.

By 1879, the US Government deemed it necessary to bring all the earth sciences together under one authority and so it established the US Geological Survey (USGS). However, it was not until the eruption of Mount St Helens, Washington State, in 1980, that the science of volcanology really started to get fully underway. This eruption provided a lot of scientific information which allowed the science to develop rapidly.

Ted Nield of the Geology Society of London explains to me that "supervolcanoes" such as the one at Yellowstone and the Campi Phlegraei near Naples, pose a significant threat to the planet. He describes Yellowstone as "quiescent" with an eruption approximately every 600 thousand years, saying that the word "dormant" does not really mean anything.

Today volcanoes are monitored in the US by the USGS, using seismic instruments to look for signs of an imminent eruption. Samples of rock, ash and debris are also studied. Thermal devices are also placed in volcanic lakes and vents in order to spot signs of possible volcanic activity. Gases emitted by volcanoes are monitored for any sign of changes that are out of the ordinary. All this information is collected by the USGS to provide advance warning of possible eruptions.

A volcanologist is generally employed by a government agency, by a university, or by private industry. They spend some of their working days out in the field, hiking through mountains whatever the weather and venturing out to the mouths of volcanoes to collect samples. But a lot of their work is done back in the lab, analysing rock samples, and they also attend scientific conferences.

Although few universities offer courses in volcanology, most scientists in this field are highly qualified with a master's degree or a PhD, often majoring in geology, earth sciences, chemistry or physics. They also study subsidiary subjects such as geophysics, geochemistry, geomorphology and petrology as well as specialist geology courses, for example in structural geology and sedimentary geology.

There are four different specialisms in volcanology. The first of these is that of the Physical Volcanologist, whose job it is to study how eruptions take place and the erupted deposits they produce, enabling them to learn about a volcano's history and helping to predict future volcanic activity. A Petrologist, meanwhile, studies the rocks and minerals that volcanoes have emitted which facilitates an understanding of the pressure and temperature of magma chambers in the earth's crust. A Geodist is a scientist who studies the physical changes that volcanoes undergo when they are erupting, while a Geochemist studies volcanoes' gaseous emission. These can be an important advance warning of an eruption, and they also affect climate change.

Volcanologists, who put their lives at risk by approaching active volcanoes, often in remote locations, are amongst science's most daring researchers, studying one of nature's harshest forces. Lorraine Field, a volcanologist who studied the Nyamuragira volcano in the Democratic Republic of Congo whilst it was erupting, described her experience to BBC News as being like "an assault on the senses".

She explained how much her life had changed over the last 10 years, when she left her desk bound job in a telecoms company for the challenges and excitement of working as a volcanologist. Having been made redundant from the office job she took up a studying full time. What had started as a career break became her dream career after she completed a BSc in Geology at Durham University followed by a PhD at Bristol as a mature student. Field currently works for the British Geological Survey and described how much she loves her job: "I can't wait to get up in the morning and come in to work now" she said. "I get excited about everything I do now – it has completely changed my life."

Visiting the volcano in the Democratic Republic of Congo was an unusual task, because unlike the practice in most of her field work, where she is looking at geology "as it happened over hundreds, thousands or even million years", this time she was studying rock that was formed as she looked on. "This was incredible. You don't often get a chance to experience that" said Field.

Studying volcanoes close up can be dangerous and many volcanologists have died attempting to do this. In 1993 six volcanologists were killed while studying the active volcano, Galeras, in Colombia, first-hand. Field had her own scrape with danger while studying the Erta Ale volcano in Ethiopia. She explained how she and her colleagues found it erupting when they reached it, which they had not expected. They got too close to the lava and had to run clear. But for Field the opportunity to travel to and study remote volcanoes is worth the risk.

Her sense of adventure is shared by fellow volcanologists such as Dr Clive Oppenheimer of Cambridge University. He visited Antarctica for one month every year to study Mount Erebus in temperatures typically of -30 degrees C (-22F). Oppenheimer told BBC News he enjoyed working in these conditions, describing it as “the closest to being an astronaut and going to Mars or somewhere very exotic”. He would ideally want to visit Jupiter’s moon Europa where there are known to be plenty of volcanoes, but for him, Antarctica is the next best thing. “You have all sorts of space suit gear to cope with the extreme weather”, he said.

Dr Oppenheimer’s research aims to find out “why some volcanoes erupt explosively whilst others erupt peacefully and why the same volcanoes sometimes switch very dramatically”, as BBC News put it. He says that scientists in the UK primarily became interested in volcanoes after the eruption in Iceland which caused European flights to be grounded, in 2011. As he said: “I think everyone needs to maybe not care about volcanoes, but certainly be interested in them”. Since people in the UK are not directly threatened by volcanoes, because of the lack of seismic activity here, the science has taken longer to become embedded in this country.

Wing-Walking

WING-WALKING DATES BACK MOSTLY TO 1920s America. The earliest known case of someone wing-walking on a powered aircraft is that of 26-year-old Ormer Locklear. Rumour has it that he first stepped outside the cockpit on to the lower wings of his biplane while he was doing his pilot's training to fix mechanical issues. In 1918 he amazed the public with his daredevil wing-walking at Barron Field, Texas. Other wing-walkers took to the skies in the US during the 1920s and tried to outdo each other. They boasted that their aim was to make money out of a spectacle in which the crowds might see them die.

The aircraft were available relatively cheaply since there was a surplus on the market of planes that had been used during World War 1. Soon after the war, wing-walking was practised by the US Army Air Corps for such activities as mid-air refuelling. In 1921, aviator Wesley May performed a plane-to-plane transfer with a fuel tank strapped to his back.

Ormer Locklear was known as the most prolific mid-air acrobat at first, but many others followed, including Ethel Dare who, true to her name, performed these daring acts. She was the first woman to switch planes mid-flight, but in 1924 she died while carrying out an aerobatic feat. During the early years of wing-walking, several people died over a relatively short time, including Locklear himself, in 1920 whilst carrying out a stunt for a film.

As the art of wing-walking developed as a spectator sport, its practitioners thought up ever more elaborate stunts, such as doing handstands, hanging by one's teeth and climbing off one plane on to another. Later, wing -walkers succeeded in transferring from a ground-based vehicle such as a car, boat or train on to a flying aircraft. Other stunts included free-falling, with the parachute only opening at the last minute.

Charles Lindbergh, who is famous for the first solo flight across the Atlantic, started his career in aviation as a wing-walker. He was shown the ropes by stunt artist Virginia Angel. The first African American woman to be granted an international pilot's licence was Bessie Coleman who also carried out parachute jumps. Lillian Boyer was a prolific female wing-walker who performed hundreds of times, including car to plane transfers and stunts using parachutes.

Groups of performers formed into "flying circuses" who advertised their daredevil exhibitions to the general public including the names of well-known performers. Many of these folded around the time of the Wall Street Crash in 1929, but some smaller operations such as the Flying Aces, run by Jimmy and Jessie Woods, survived. In 1938 the US Air Commerce Act compelled wing-walkers to wear parachutes. Legislation was also passed in the 1930s to ban wing-walking below 1,500 ft (457 metres), effectively ending it as a spectator sport in the US.

During the 1970s, with the rules relaxed, there was something of a revival in wing-walking there. Ron David, himself a gifted aviator, took control of the Flying Circus at Bealeton, Virginia and returned it to its old tradition of daring aerobatics. In 1981 an unofficial wing-walking world record was set by a group of 19 skydivers who all stood together of one wing of an aircraft.

In the US today, as well as in other countries, including the UK, wing-walking continues to be done by a small number of people. The show is much like it always was, save for the fact that a safety harness must be worn. There is a lot of glamour associated with wing-walking these days, of which AeroSuperBatics Wingwalkers are a prime example. This British team, with their bright orange Boeing Stearman aircraft and their good-looking female aerobats, have been described as "the only formation display team in the world". They were formerly known as the Breitling

Wingwalkers because of the association they had with the Swiss watch manufacturer.

At the time of writing the team consists of three women, Sarah Tanner, Danielle Hughes and Stella Guilding. Based at RFC Rendcomb in the Cotswolds, a former WW1 airfield, they "spend the summer months performing complicated loops, handstands and rolls, 1000 ft (305 metres) above ground, attached to a mainframe harness and a few bits of cable", as the *Guardian* puts it. They are watched by around six million spectators per year in the UK alone, according to the *Guardian*. This can be at air shows, charity or corporate events and special occasions, including weddings.

The Stearman is a popular choice of aircraft with wing-walkers, because it is relatively slow and stable with aerobatic capability. Despite this the aerial acrobats face speeds of up to 150 miles (241 km) per hour and g-forces of up to 4g, which means they experience gravity at four times its normal strength.

Although not many airfields have the equipment and training services needed, a few companies in the UK offer wing-walking experiences to the public. AeroSuperBatics is one of these. They describe the ride as one of being on the wing during flypasts, zoom climbs, steep dives and banks, while awe-struck family and friends look on. From 2019 the company also offers the chance to fly with a partner on another plane, including flying side by side and zooming past each other. Another company offering such experiences to the public is Into the Blue, which operates from three airfields in the UK. Staff at these aerodromes are on hand to train people up for a wing-walk in a very short time. One example of what they must learn is that of the hand signals used to communicate with the pilot. These are deployed because a wing-walker cannot hear the pilot speak due to the sound of the wind passing by.

The airfields used must also offer the essential kit for wing-walking such as a bespoke safety harness which can only be provided with a significant cost. Safety is paramount and the UK has strict rules around wing-walking.

Few wing-walkers get as much joy out of the experience as did Margi Stivers who worked with her pilot husband Hartley Folstad on their reconditioned Stearman planes, for 20 years leading up to 2011. They were based in California and thrilled air-show audiences across the country.

After meeting in the 1980s, they took on the roles of successors to the barnstorming aerial acrobats of the 1920s. They carried out 15-minute aerial performances which wowed the crowds with their daring aerobatics and ballet style manoeuvres by Stivers, which involved a good deal of trust between the acrobat and the pilot.

As Stivers told *airportjournals.com*: "I had this gift inside me that I never opened until that first moment I climbed out of the cockpit." She went on to say: "By allowing myself to open this gift, I also get to share it with others." Stivers first ventured out on to the wings of an aircraft in 1991, but it was not until more recently that the pair's act has seriously got underway. They began as part of the Silver Wings Wingwalking Team, which consisted of a team of three to five Stearman planes working together with wing-walkers on board. But more recently they have worked as a solo act. Over this time, Stivers, a trained dancer and acrobat, developed her act into a selection of incredible moves which she carried out "on the wings of a moving biplane – sometimes at speeds approaching 100 miles an hour", according to *airportjournals.com*. This was done with great courage on her part and great skill by her husband.

Pilots as well as wing-walkers must practise daily, but for Stivers and Folstad the effort was worthwhile because of the joy their amazing profession gave them.

Xylography

XYLOGRAPHY IS THE ART OF wood cut printing where the image is carved into a block of wood. The printing areas are level with the surface and the non-printing areas gouged away with a knife or chisel. Ink is applied to the surface of the block, using an ink roller, so that the surface will be printed without the non-printing areas.

This technique of printing from wood carvings existed in ancient China but became known in Europe by the latter part of the fourteenth century. This was at about the same time as people started to use paper, which was better suited to the printing process than parchment. Manuscript writers used this method to decorate the initial capital letters of a book or document. This saved a considerable amount of time in a process which had previously been done by hand for each individual manuscript.

Attempts were made to create movable type from woodcuts in the 1420s and 1430s, but the type made in this way was fragile and wore out quickly. Since the letters were carved by hand, no two pieces of type of the same letter were exactly alike. The process proved to be no easier, quicker or more effective than carving blocks in the traditional way.

The process of xylography requires skill, simple tools and planning. Although it has its origins in ancient China it proved very useful to manuscript writers in Europe in late medieval times to illustrate their texts. In Japan it is known as 'muku hanga' and was developed in the seventeenth century for colour prints in books and art.

Multiple colours can be printed using a separate block for each colour.

According to *historygraphicdesign.com*: "Coloured wood cuts first appeared in China. The oldest known are three Buddhist images dating from the tenth century". Using coloured blocks for printing emerged in Europe in early sixteenth century Germany, but printing in colour did not become the norm in Europe as it did later in Japan.

Chinese colour woodcuts appeared most frequently in top notch books about art. The earliest known example of this is a book published in 1606 and the use of colour in xylography reached its peak in books about paintings there later in the seventeenth century. "Notable examples are Hu Zhengyan's *Treatise on the Paintings and Writings of the Ten Bamboo Studio* of 1633 and the *Mustard Seed Garden Painting Manual* published in 1679 and 1701" (*historygraphicdesign.com*).

For the wood cut process, an artist would first create the image to be followed by the wood cutter. This division of labour meant that the artist could easily adapt to the medium without the need to acquire woodworking skills. However, in ancient China, those people involved in the production of such prints were seen as artisans rather than artists. By the twentieth century in Japan and China, as well as in Europe, artists increasingly chose to make the wood blocks themselves. Sometimes European artists would create lino cuts instead.

There were various ways that the artist's drawing could be transferred to the wood cut. This was either done by the artist drawing directly on to the block, or a drawing on paper was fixed to it. Either way the artist's drawing did not survive the process. A number of other methods were sometimes used, such as tracing.

Unlike in etching and engraving, only light pressure needs to be applied to the printing block. It is only necessary to ink the block and place it on to the paper or cloth. The wood of choice in Europe was generally fruit wood such as pear or cherry, while "in Japan the wood of the cherry species 'Prunus serrulata' was preferred" (*historygraphicdesign.com*).

The early European method was simply to ink the blocks and apply them to the paper, but in ancient China and Japan, the rubbing method was used instead. This process migrated to Europe in the late fifteenth century and by the early twentieth century was used widely here. With this printing method, the block is placed face-up with the fabric or paper placed on top. The back of this surface is rubbed with a flat instrument such as a piece of wood or a leather frotton.

In Japan, for colour printing, complex wooden mechanisms were used to hold the wood blocks in place and to apply the necessary pressure to create a part of the image, in a particular colour. It took much precision to arrange the multiple colour images so that they fitted together in the end product.

Printing presses using movable type were not used in the ancient Far East but were introduced to Europe in about 1450 by Johannes Gutenberg. These provided competition for the wood cut process of making prints as well as being invaluable for book printing.

Printing using wood cuts came to Europe significantly earlier than the invention of the printing presses. A profusion of cheap woodcuts came on to the market in the mid-fifteenth century which meant that standards of the craft declined with many crude prints becoming available. In 1475, however, Michael Wolgemut was making more sophisticated wood cuts in what is now Germany. "At the end of the century" as *historygraphicdesign.com* puts it, "Albrecht Durer brought the Western woodcut to a level that, arguably, has never been surpassed." This greatly increased the status of the single wood cut. Wood cuts were used to illustrate manuscripts until the late sixteenth century. The use of xylography for fine-art prints declined in Europe after 1550 but underwent something of a revival in the nineteenth century.

In Japan the colour block printing process, known as nishiki-e, was used more widely than it was in China, mostly for prints, from 1760 onwards. Both in the Far East and in Europe, book illustrations and text were usually monochrome, but there was increasing demand in Japan for ever more colourful and complex prints. In nishiki-e the separate colour blocks were used to create highly detailed, multi-coloured images, put together with great care using registration marks called kento.

The full colour method developed in Japan during the late eighteenth century continued to thrive through the twentieth century. By then xylography had become a major artistic medium, usually produced in colour, although it was held in lower esteem than that of painting.

In the 1860s, just as the Japanese were becoming more interested in western art, their wood cut prints started to appear in Europe and soon became very fashionable, especially in France. This work influenced French artists such as Manet, Toulouse-Lautrec, Degas and Gauguin. In 1872 this trend was dubbed 'le Japonisme' by Jules Claretie, a French literary figure and director of the Theatre Francais.

As Japanese xylography brought influence to bear on European art in general in the late nineteenth century, there was a revival of European wood-cut artwork, which had formerly been in serious decline.

Japan today is known for its technological innovations but there are still people who cling to their cultural roots. The process of making a wood cut is the same as it always was, save the one modern addition to the workshop, the electric lamp.

Yeomen Warders

THESE ARE ONE OF THE most popular attractions for visitors to the Tower of London. Known as Beefeaters they are traditional symbols of Britain and of London in particular. They are the ceremonial guards of the Tower. In theory their job is to look after any prisoners there and to guard the Crown Jewels. The last famous prisoner was Rudolf Hess, the Nazi Deputy Chancellor who strangely flew to Scotland during WW2 in a bid to speak to the British government. He was kept in the Tower as late as 1941.

Since Victorian times, Beefeaters have mainly conducted guided tours of the Tower. One of their number is appointed Ravenmaster or Yeoman Warder Ravenmaster, who is responsible for the ravens at the Tower. A chapter in this book is devoted to this job in its own right.

According to website of Historic Royal Palaces, the independent charity which looks after the Tower, the origin of the name "Beefeater" is thought to be derived from the fact that, historically, they were allowed "to eat as much beef as they wanted from the King's table". They have guarded the Tower since at least 1509 and the reign of Henry VII. It was then that the King moved his official residence from the Tower to Hampton Court Palace, leaving behind a small garrison of 12 Beefeaters. There has been at least a dozen of them, led by a Chief Yeoman Warder, guarding the Tower ever since. It is thought that their origins date back to the reign of Edward IV (1461-83).

The Beefeaters are sometimes referred to as the "Yeomen of the Guard", the Royal bodyguard, who were the subject of Gilbert and Sullivan's operetta of the same name. This was set in the sixteenth century, before the Yeoman Warders became a separate detachment. Both wear an almost identical ceremonial uniform which, as *projectbritain.com* describes it: "consists of a knee-length scarlet tunic, scarlet knee breeches and stockings and a round brimmed hat called a Tudor bonnet". The distinctive white neck ruff was introduced by Queen Elizabeth I. The Yeomen of the Guard can only be distinguished from the Yeomen Warders by their cross belts worn from the left shoulder. For everyday duties the Beefeaters wear a red and dark blue uniform known as an "undress uniform" which was granted to them by Queen Victoria in 1858.

Although the Beefeaters today have a friendly and respectable image, centuries ago they had a reputation for drunkenness, disorders and quarrels. In 1598, Sir John Peyton, the Lieutenant of the Tower, criticised them for their rather sleazy reputation.

As described by the *Guardian,* historian Dr Jeanette Martin has conducted research into the Beefeaters at the Tower of London and their place in British identity. She discovered that unlike those of today, in previous centuries the Beefeaters were "a shocking bunch of scoundrels in urgent need of reform", as the *Guardian* puts it. An eighteenth-century tourist would have been well advised to beware of extortionate Beefeaters plying their trade as tour guides.

As the contemporary writer John Bayley put it in his book *The History and Antiquities of the Tower of London*: "Rather than guarding the tower they have gradually assumed to themselves the more lucrative occupation of stopping everybody who wishes to visit these objects of our national pride and glory and forcing themselves upon them as their guides."

Fortunately for the tourists of later centuries, the Duke of Wellington was appointed as the Tower's new constable in 1826 and soon got to work improving the attitude and behaviour of the Beefeaters. "This involved sacking the worst incumbents and abolishing the practice of Beefeaters selling on their positions to anyone who had a spare 250 guineas", according to the *Guardian.*

Today the role is restricted to those who have a track record of 22 years military service and who have achieved the rank of Warrant Officer or above. They are also required to have received a good conduct medal. These are some of the rules that Wellington introduced. The job is salaried, but the warders are nowadays employed by Historic Royal Palaces. The Beefeaters pay a market rent for their accommodation within the grounds of the Tower and must own another property to which to retire. The Tower community of residents is comprised of various officials and their families, consisting of the Beefeaters, the Residential Governor and officers, a chaplain and a doctor.

Although it may not have been one of his intentions, Wellington's reforms democratised the roll resulting in any man "however low his origins, through long and exemplary service in the army, being able to obtain this prized position". (The *Guardian*). Since the military were drawn from all over the UK, the Beefeaters could be recruited from all four of its home nations.

New recruits take part in a drinking ceremony held at the Beefeaters' drinking club, as a form of initiation. They are given a special goblet and a toast is made in their honour which goes as follows: "May you never die a Yeoman Warder". This dates back to the days when they could sell on their office.

The first woman to be appointed as a Beefeater was Moira Cameron, in 2007. She joined the Army in 1985 at the age of 20. Suitably qualified, she became a Beefeater at the age of 42. The fact that, at the time of writing, there is only one female Beefeater reflects the lack of women in the armed services who have 22 years' experience. Although the number of female recruits is growing rapidly, 20 years ago their number was much smaller than it is today. It will be a while yet before a large cohort of female Beefeaters greet tourists at the Tower.

The job of Beefeater is a sought after one, despite the fact that the tourists tend to ask uninteresting questions, the most frequently asked one being "Where's the toilet?". "When they leave the army" observes Martin, "they are still relatively young". She says the job offers them security and the chance to keep away from conflict zones. As she puts it: "After you've had a career going around the world, the world comes to you."

Working as a Beefeater is a somewhat quirky job with its age-old formalities such as the ceremony of the keys, which they carry out every night. This is a ritual that has been carried out for about 700 years and is concerned with the locking up of the Tower at night. It is believed to be the longest standing military ceremony in the world and is the best-known tradition of the Beefeaters. There is also a tradition that because of an old agreement with Marston to use the Beefeater image on their gin bottles, they are given free gin on special occasions, for example their birthdays.

Another oddity that one of them described to Martin was that as he did the washing up, he looked out at the spot where many executions took place, including that of Anne Boleyn. The job does not stop when the site is closed to tourists for the day and part of the traditional duties of the Beefeaters has always been to guard the Tower at night.

During the 1930s, during a civil service industrial dispute, the Beefeaters went on strike and were not available to assist tourists but continued to guard the Tower at night and donated what they were paid to do this to charity.

Beefeaters have gone from being a disreputable bunch of rascals for centuries to being, in the modern day, a respectable symbol of Britishness. But what goes on late at night in their private drinking club, is something the public may never know.

Zinco-printing

ZINCO-PRINTING OR PHOTO-ZINCOGRAPHY IS DERIVED from an earlier process known as zincography, which was a printing process using zinc plates. Zincography was patented by Federico Lacelli in 1834 and used to create large maps called georamas. It was improved upon by Eugene Florent Kaeppelin between 1837 and 1842.

Zinc plates were less costly than lithographic limestone and could be made to a very large size. The zinc was coated with acids and a complicated process was carried out using various chemicals which resulted in the creation of a printing proof.

Zincography is often confused with the more modern process of photo-zincography, known as "zinco-printing". Photo-zincography is a process that involves the use of a zinc plate treated with a mixture of salts and other substances, exposed in contact with a positive paper proof created from a glass negative.

The process of zinco-printing was developed under the direction of Sir Henry James FRS (1803-1877) in the mid-nineteenth century. Sir Henry was Director General of the British Ordnance Survey which was responsible for publishing map series, including the 1:2500 and 1:500 versions. Zinco-printing allowed printers to accurately reproduce images, manuscript text and outline engravings. According to cartographers' website *gislounge.com*, it was "a revolutionary way of copying photographic negatives on to zinc", that was, "in a sense, the first photocopying machine produced". This made the reproduction of maps, photographs and literary works much easier and it proved invaluable for the Ordnance Survey of Great Britain.

Zinco-printing enabled the Ordnance Survey to reproduce large-scale maps much more cheaply than the earlier method, of engraving on copper. However, the first use of photography by the Ordnance Survey was to enable scale-changing, to enable smaller scale maps to be produced from the basic large-scale surveys. Despite concern that photography would distort the map image, Sir Henry pressed ahead, setting up a photography department at the Ordnance Survey in 1855, having secured funding to set up and run a photography building with a glass roof, in order to maximise available light.

It was four years later that the idea of photo-zincography arose, being mentioned by Sir Henry in his report to Parliament in 1859. Initially the process was unable to produce negatives large enough for maps of the "double-elephant" 6-inch maps (91.4 by 61 cm) size or larger, due to fact that this required larger negatives than those that were currently available. This meant that initially only non-standard maps were produced by this method, and that when from 1881 the six-inch (1:10,560) maps were produced by photo-zincography, they had to be issued in quarter-sheet size (45.7 by 30.5 cm). Because of this lack of suitable negatives, the use of zinco for domestic map production was at first rather limited. Its main use in the 1860s was for the reproduction of historical manuscripts, such as the Domesday Book which was copied in 1861-4, to make them accessible to the public.

By the 1870s the process had been sufficiently improved to allow its use for the rapid production of overseas maps for the War Office. From 1881-2, zinco-printing was used on a significant scale to speed up the production of domestic 6-inch (1:10,560) maps, which had previously been engraved.

By 1889 cameras and negatives were available that enabled zinco-printing to be used for full size "double-elephant" sheets. Although Sir Henry claimed to have invented the process, a similar idea was patented in Australia by John Walter Osborne (1828-1902), but Sir Henry pointed out to him that he had publicised his version first. However, it was not Sir Henry who invented the process of zinco-printing. Captain Alexander de Courcy

Scott along with his assistant Lance Corporal Ryder working under Sir Henry at the Ordnance Survey in Southampton, were responsible for much of the development of the idea. But Sir Henry took most of the credit and was knighted in 1861 for his services to science.

The main improvement over lithographic printing was that photo-zincography did not require the use of stones. Zinc plates were lighter and less brittle which made them easier to transport, without the risk of them shattering, as stones were prone to do. They could be used to produce more copies and their use led to the term "photo-zincography", an invention that Sir Henry James claimed credit for.

The introduction of zinco-printing to the Ordnance Survey proved very successful, and saved much money, especially with maps of urban areas, making it nine times cheaper for maps of this kind. It was also claimed that a single image could be reproduced 2,000-3,000 times. However, the result did have its imperfections. It did not reproduce a full colour image, and well into the twentieth century some maps were hand coloured. This was a time-consuming exercise. The popularity of zinco-printing spread rapidly to the continent. Sir Henry even received an honour from the Queen of Spain.

By 1892 an alternative to zinco-printing had been developed, known as helio-zincography. As Richard Oliver of the Charles Close Society, an organisation dedicated to the study of Ordnance Survey maps, explains: "The essential difference between the two was that what was sometimes known as the helio-process worked by placing the photographic negative directly in contact with the sensitised zinc plate", which avoided the necessity of the transfer process needed in photozincography. Helio-zincography and photo-zincography were both used for the manufacture of large-scale maps in large quantities from the 1800s to the 1930s, but it is helio-zincography which is better known.

Helio-zincography soon became the dominant of the two processes for the production of 6 inch (15.2 cm), 1:2500 maps and larger scale maps. Yet, because of the storage space needed for the negatives and plates of both these processes, they were used sparingly at the larger scale.

In 1900 a new method devised by Conductor Vandyke of the Survey of India became available. This method, known as "Vandyking", had several advantages: it was a photographic method which did not require the use of a camera or a negative, and the thin zinc plates used took up less storage space that the bulkier plates and glass negatives used before this time.

The use of zinco-printing started to diminish from the late 1880s as new methods proved more economical and during the 1900s the glasshouse was demolished, to make way for new printing presses. But Richard Oliver explains to me that the process continued to be used until more recently to produce maps, posters and other "illustrative material".

Acknowledgements

2-clicks-coins
A Dictionary of Old Trades, Titles and Occupations – Colin Waters
Aerosuperbatics
Airport Journals
Akvis.com
Alert Diver
Alex McRae
Amusing Planet
Ancient Pages.com
APMEX
Association of Foragers
Association of Psychological Science
Atlasobscura.com
Aweski.com
Backstage
BBC
Beach Huts and Bathing Machines– Kathryn Ferry
Beachcombing's Bizarre History blog
Beerandbrewing.com
BigPicture
BNT.org.uk
Bognor-local-history.co.uk
Boing Boing
Britannica.com
Bruichladdich Whisky

Buildingconservation.com
Built Landscape Heritage Education & Training Project
Careeraddict.com
Carynshulenberg.com
Centralbedfordshire.gov.uk
Cerbomentia.com
Ceredigion County Council
Charles Close Society
Cheekyumbrella.com
Chef's Blade
Chertsey Museum
Chris Bullzini
City of London Corporation
Colonial Quills
Comitti
Connectedstudios.org
Connorslegacy.co.uk
Constructorscompany.org.uk
Coracle Society
Cork Dork: a wine fuelled journey into the art of Master Sommeliers and the science of taste -Bianca Bosker
Crossref.it.info
Cumbria County Council
Daily Mail
Data Wales
David McConaghay
Deanverders.org.uk
Decanter
Decodedpast.com
Digging History
Dominion Post
Donnahatch.com
Dylan Jones
Englishhistoryauthors.blogspot.co.uk
Environmentalscience.org
Espn.com
Fashiontime.org/history

Fast company

Field Journals

Financial Times

For Crying out Loud :The Story of the Town Crier and Bellman, Past and Present – David Mitchell

Forest Law and the Verderers of the New Forest -Sarah Neild

Garethjonesfood.com

Genealogy Research Network

Geological Society of London

Geriwalton.com

GIS Lounge

Go Think Big

Golf Today

Golfballdivers.com

Gradulthood Jobs

Graphics.com

Heretic Magazine

Hermitary.com

Hermits.ex.ac.uk

Historic Royal Palaces

Historic UK

History of Graphic Design

Historyhouse.co.uk

Historyofphrenology.org

HowStuffWorks

Ideal Shanghai

Ilford Photo

Incentivetravel.co.uk

Industry and Business

Inside Jobs

Into the Blue

Jane Austen's world

Jobmonkey.com

Julie Rees

Katie Marshall

Kaufmann-mercantile.com

KnowledgeNuts

Lancashire Life

Like2do.com

Liverpool Museums

Livescience.com

Lizzie Rivera

London Characters and Crooks-Henry Mayhew

London Evening Standard

London Lives

London Metropolitan Archive

Londonist

Lucinda Brandt -English Historical Fiction Authors

Mark Dellar

Market Watch

Mentalfloss

Metro News

Monet Pantry

Monitor

My Job Hub Blog

National Geographic

National Portrait Gallery

Neatorama

Odditycentral.com

Paul Cox

Payscale.com

Pbs.com

Period Property UK

Perukes & Periwigs (National Portrait Gallery)

Photography Forum

Pit Brow Lasses. Who Were They?

Projectbritain.com

Psychology Today

QI Quite Interesting

Ranker.com

Reaktionsburo Mathais Meier

Religionfacts.com

Rhymer Rigby

Richard Oliver

Royal Numismatists Society
Science Museum
Sciencing
Scubadiving.com
Sealy Posuturepedic
Shipsandoil.com
Sky News
Smithsonian Institute
Sokanu.com
Spitalfields Life
Stephen Freeth
Steve Hiemhoff Blog
Straits Times
Streetdirectory.com
Sussexlietenancy.org.uk
Sustainable Food Trust
Ted Neild
Telegraph.co.uk
Tetley Tea Academy
Theabracadabra
The Birth of the British Bobby. Bow Street Runners, Scotland Yard & Victorian Crime -Don Hale OBE
Theartcareerproject.com
Thebeadlesoflondon.com
The Catholic Encyclopedia
The Cochineal
Thecompassnews.org
The Guardian
The Illustrated History of Magic - Milbourne and Maurice Christopher
Theimportanceofbeingtrivial.com
The Independent
The New Encyclopedia
The New Yorker
Theoldfoodie.com
The Penny Hoarder
Thespruce.com
Thoughtco

Time Magazine
Totallyhistory.com
Tower of London
Trinity College Library, Cambridge
Umbrellahistory.net
Unblinkingeye.com
United Photograph Artists Gallery
Universe Today
Unusual Historicals
Urbanhistory.net
Vannessaairely.com/blog
Verderers.co.uk
Victoria and Albert Museum
Visual-arts-cork.com
Wales online
What Could I Wear Today?
Wikipedia
Winshipwalking.co.uk
Wizegeek.com
Wolverhampton History
Women in Mining Communities
Workshopsforschools.co.uk
World of Psychology
Woven Communities
Yourlocalguardian.com
Zythropia.co.uk

Biographical Note – John McKie

JOHN MCKIE IS A SOCIAL Science graduate from the Open University. He has worked for a number of organisations in the not-for-profit sector including Macmillan Cancer Support and the NHS, and from 2013 as a grants administrator for the D.M.Thomas Foundation. His interests include science, sociology, photography, the environment, world news and classical music.

Printed in Great Britain
by Amazon